Praise for
Dr. Steven R. Edgley and *Thriving After Your Stroke*

"Having watched my mother cope with a wheelchair after her back operation went terribly wrong, I understand how vitally important it is to learn to accept and adapt when life throws you curves. This remarkable book explores this concept while offering sound and practical advice (backed by proven principles) that bring hope and enlightenment in the direst of circumstances. Dr. Edgley deeply understands what lies ahead of stroke victims and their families, and he provides a path to help them realistically recreate meaningful lives. A truly valuable and tremendous book!"

— Stephen M. R. Covey, *The New York Times* Bestselling Author of *The Speed of Trust*

"'I don't think Steve will survive this,' I said to his father as we stood at the foot of his bed where Steve lay unconscious and motionless after a massive stroke. I was never so glad to be wrong. In fact, my good friend, Steve Edgley, not only recovered, but with incredible determination, relearned his speech, regained his ability to walk, and became an honor medical student, resident, and now university professor. He has become an example for hundreds of people in rehabilitation, and he is now advancing the fields for stroke and brain injury recovery."

— Scott J. Kolbaba, MD, *Chicago Magazine* Top Doctor and Author of the Amazon Bestseller *Physicians' Untold Stories*

"I felt alone until I came to realize Dr. Edgley had the same kind of stroke I'd had and had experienced the same thing I was going through. His compassion and understanding was immeasurable. He understands what it is like because he has gone through the hard work of regaining walking ability and arm recovery, as well as speech and language recovery. During my hospital stay and afterwards, he has continued to be an inspiration that recovery and happiness in life are possible after a stroke."

— Craig M. Marsh, Stroke Survivor

"In *Thriving After Your Stroke*, Steve Edgley speaks with the authority of personal experience. He has 'been there and done that.' I know his family well and I have a lot of respect for how he dealt with his own stroke. He fought through it, grew from it as a person, and ultimately built a new life for himself and his family.

"Now, in *Thriving After Your Stroke*, he offers hope, encouragement, and practical advice for regaining the ability to thrive for stroke patients and their loved ones. However, I would add that this book is truly impactful for any audience. It is a metaphor for the overall universal human experience. It is a road map on how to meet head-on the challenges that life throws at us, with grace and grit, and come out the other side a better human being, better able to impact the lives of others. I recommend it for anyone who is faced with a seemingly overwhelming challenge in their life."

— Hyrum W. Smith, Cofounder of FranklinCovey, Author of *What Matters Most*, CEO, The Galileo Initiative

"Besides being a great stroke rehabilitation specialist, Dr. Steven Edgley is a fine human being. When you meet him, it is obvious that he has a slow speech pattern and his right hand is a bit impaired. Though he could consider himself 'disabled' from these limitations, he is not disabled at all. Dr. Edgley has chosen *ability* as his way of life. It is through his life story of ability that Dr. Edgley provides a pathway to follow for those who have suffered stroke. It is a story of success over cure, of life over survival."

— Richard L. Harvey, MD, Clinical Chair, Brain Innovation Center, Shirley Ryan AbilityLab, Chicago, Illinois

"This is a remarkable book for people who have experienced a stroke, and for those who love and care for them. But the relevance of the story goes far beyond this group. During our lives, we all experience trying situations we never dreamed we would face. How do we respond to these crises? How do we heal ourselves and go forward? The principles taught in this inspiring book are for all of us who sojourn through the drama of life. I highly recommend it!"

— Michael Glauser, PhD, Author of *Main Street Entrepreneur*, Executive Director of the Center for Entrepreneurship, Jon M. Huntsman School of Business at Utah State University

"Perhaps the most remarkable of all is not that Dr. Edgley has overcome his own stroke and has dedicated his entire existence to helping patients, friends and colleagues to overcome their own strokes, but it is that he now THRIVES in his own life, not ever succumbing to being any sort of victim. His story will inspire you to live beyond the bounds of what you currently think is possible."

— James Clarke, CEO of Clarke Capital Partners, Chair of Foundation Board & Trustee, Utah Valley University

"Steve has walked with faith and hope through some of life's most difficult paths. His ability to inspire others with his genuine words makes this book a must read. You will have more hope in your daily life by letting the pages of this book lift you above your own challenges!"

— Chad Lewis, Former NFL All-Pro Player, Author of *Surround Yourself With Greatness*, and Current BYU Associate Athletic Director

"In this book, Dr. Steve Edgley poignantly describes the challenges that occurred when a devastating stroke forever changed his expected trajectory in life. In this book, he vividly expresses how his steadfast faith provided him a stable foundation from which to rebuild his life and the strength and insight not only to endure but excel. As someone who was privileged to work with this extraordinary physician, I witnessed how his humbling experience magnified his compassion and empathy for others. This inspiring book highlights the power of personal choices, perseverance, and focused resolve in transforming a tragedy into a blessing, even a gift. For anyone experiencing a heartrending misfortune in life, it is a touching and stirring message of hope after adversity."

— Phillip R. Bryant, DO, Former Division Chief of Physical Medicine and Rehabilitation, University of Utah, Current Division Chief at the Children's Hospital of Philadelphia

"Steve's story is a remarkable one of faith, family, and courage allowing him to overcome a devastating stroke and become a physician who uses his life lessons to care for others. Having been one of Steve's medical school teachers and honored to assist Steve when he was recovering, I thank God for his life and know this book will inspire many."

— Rev. Myles N. Sheehan, SJ, MD, Current Provincial of the New England Province of the Jesuits and Former Senior Associate Dean at the Stritch School of Medicine of Loyola University of Chicago

"Dr. Edgley helped me through some very difficult times in my recovery from a stroke I sustained in September of 2013. He let me know that there are brighter days through the tunnel of life. He is just one of those 'lead-by-example' individuals. Dr. Edgley was absolutely vital to my recovery. His zest for enjoyment of life is contagious. He is more than a doctor—he is a true friend."

— Brian Hultman, Attorney, Stroke Survivor, and Ted-X Lecturer, Jackson, Wyoming

"Dr. Steven Edgley has a unique gift. On a daily basis, he can relate to exactly what his patients are experiencing. Edgley himself suffered stroke at age 28. He quickly changed his career path and is now the Director of the Stroke Rehabilitation Program at the University of Utah."

— Utah Business Editors, "Healthcare Heroes,"
Utah Business Magazine, October 2013

"Steven Edgley's story inspires on every level. Already intending to become a doctor, his stroke ended up directing his life path to help other stroke sufferers reclaim their lives. This book is filled with not only medical advice but compassion and true stories of triumph. Anyone who has had a stroke or loves someone struggling with overcoming one will find hope and strength in these pages."

— Tyler Tichelaar, PhD and Award-Winning Author
of *When Teddy Came to Town*

"If anyone knows what it means to choose your own destiny, it is Steven Edgley. Even after a stroke, we all have a choice to make. In *Thriving After Your Stroke*, he shows how we can choose to be the hunter and not the prey…how we can learn to adapt to and even conquer many of the limitations that a stroke places upon us. This book is a true testament to the human spirit."

— Patrick Snow, Publishing Coach and International Bestselling
Author of *Creating Your Own Destiny* and *Boy Entrepreneur*

"In *Thriving After Your Stroke*, Dr. Steven Edgley shares the hard truths about stroke, then shares how he and the many patients he has worked with have not let those truths stand in their way but have transformed them into their own truths about themselves and what they are capable of despite all the odds. This book is a heartwarming tear-jerker about stroke and the aftermath that is possible."

— Nicole Gabriel, Author of *Finding Your Inner
Truth* and *Stepping Into Your Becoming*

A ROADMAP FOR STROKE SURVIVORS AND
THOSE WHO LOVE THEM

THRIVING AFTER YOUR STROKE

REBUILDING THE MIND AND BODY
TO CREATE A MEANINGFUL LIFE

STEVEN R. EDGLEY, MD

AVIVA
PUBLISHING
New York

Thriving After Your Stroke: Rebuilding the Mind and Body to Create a Meaningful Life

Copyright © 2019 by Steven R. Edgley. All rights reserved.

Published by:
Aviva Publishing
Lake Placid, NY, USA
(515) 523-1320
www.AvivaPubs.com

All Rights Reserved. No part of this book may be used or reproduced in any manner whatsoever without the expressed written permission of the author. Address all inquiries to:

Steven R. Edgley, MD
801-833-7457
Steve.Edgley@gmail.com
www.ThrivingAfterYourStroke.com

ISBN: 978-1-947937-93-2
Library of Congress Control Number: 2019911838

Editor: Tyler Tichelaar, Superior Book Productions
Cover Design and Interior Book Layout: Nicole Gabriel, Angel Dog Productions
Author Photo: Matthew Clayton

Every attempt has been made to source properly all quotes.
Printed in the United States of America

To my daughters, Ella and Louisa,

May you find strength, courage, and ultimately joy amid life's challenges.

And to the countless survivors who, day in and day out, persevere amid struggle and fight the good fight to build for themselves a better future on the adaptive spiral.

ACKNOWLEDGMENTS

I give thanks to my wife, Emi, for her support and for allowing me the freedom to pursue this meaningful project.

To Stacey Fiala for the valued context editing and proofreading.

To Pat Goodin for her her proofreading and valuable insights into complex social and psychological factors. To Rachel Motschiedler for her encouragement and insights. To Suzanne Stensaas for generously providing her expertise in neuroanatomy and in context editing. To Hyrum Smith for teaching me principles of goal achievement in my youth.

My gratitude goes to Patrick Snow for walking me through this publishing process, for coaching me, and for his insightful encouragement. I give thanks to Tyler Tichelaar for his dedicated and professional editing. My gratitude also goes to Nicole Gabriel for the cover design and interior layout.

Also, thanks goes to David Steinberg and Candace Floyd for their encouragement and vision. Thanks are also due to Marcia Edgley Packer for her quiet example of resilience and fortitude amid significant lifelong impairments.

Finally, thanks goes to Brian Hultman, Craig Marsh, Courtenay Marvin, David Rich, Coby Bascom, Helen Thiriot, and Tim Gamble; also, all of the unnamed patients who inspire me

With deep gratitude, I acknowledge my parents, Pauline and Richard Edgley, for their profound influence on my life and on my thinking.

CONTENTS

Introduction		17
Chapter 1	The Crisis That Would Define My Life	23
Chapter 2	Silence	31
Chapter 3	Doing the Hard Things and Rising	39
Chapter 4	Conquering the Mind	47
Chapter 5	When a Door Closes, Build a New One	57
Chapter 6	Hunter and Prey	63
Chapter 7	What Is "Stroke"? Demystifying the Myths	73
Chapter 8	Prevention and New Frontiers	81
Chapter 9	Language Center: The Rocket Scientist and the Eloquent Tissue of the Brain	91
Chapter 10	Wernicke's Aphasia and the Cowboy Poet	99
Chapter 11	Cognitive Syndromes After Stroke: Right Brain Syndromes	107
Chapter 12	Despite Chance Events, You Can Make Your Mark	117
Chapter 13	Surrounding Yourself With Great Resources: Critical Collaborations	125
Chapter 14	Complications After a Stroke: Gorillas and Frogs	137
Chapter 15	Adaptive Spiral and the Plastic Brain	145
Chapter 16	Spasticity and the Freedom to Move	155

Chapter 17	Stroke in the Young: Unique Issues of Driving, Working, and Other Aspects	165
Chapter 18	Stages of Life and Loss, and the Potential to Repurpose Loss for Good	177
Chapter 19	Resilience	187
Chapter 20	Nature's Restorative Power	195
Chapter 21	Caregivers of Stroke Patients: Unsung Heroes	203
Chapter 22	When End of Life Approaches	213
A Final Note:	The Adaptive Spiral Revisited	221
Bibliography		225
End Notes		231
Index		239
About the Author		245
If You Benefited From *Thriving After Your Stroke*, Don't Miss Reading *Life Between Two Gardens*		247
Book Steven Edgley to Speak at Your Next Event		249

No difficulty can discourage, no obstacle dismay, no trouble dishearten the man who has acquired the art of being alive. Difficulties are but dares of fate, obstacles but hurdles to try his skill, troubles but bitter tonics to give him strength; and he rises higher and looms greater after each encounter with adversity.

— Ella Wheeler Wilcox

INTRODUCTION

We all experience difficult things, but few things are as difficult as the life-altering struggle to regain your life after suffering a stroke. Imagine the life you've built up is like a beautiful house—a house suddenly burning down. The flames are destroying everything in their path. You have just seconds to get out and grab your valuables. In this moment of crisis, what will you take? A family heirloom? A laptop computer or a cellphone? Picture albums? Documents? What precious items will you leave behind? Often in a fire, you don't get a lot of choice regarding what to save. A stroke is a devastating life event, leaving few things but ashes. In its destructive path, the stroke will engulf nearly everything of significance to you. Your talents. Your speech. Your hobbies and interests. Your livelihood. Your physical appearance. Your dignity. You will be forced to ask yourself, given the loss of these seemingly precious things, is life still worth living? Or is your core, your "essence," comprised of something much deeper?

My metaphorical house burned to the ground on December 7, 2001, when I had a devastating stroke and nearly everything of meaning to me was destroyed. I was twenty-eight years old, a husband, a father, a resident-doctor, an athlete, a Christian. My music was still in me; my race had not yet been run. I thought I was one of the good guys so I would be safe from such an event. But a stroke, like many tragedies in life, is no respecter of persons; it literally and figuratively burned everything in its wake. It didn't matter that I was young and fit, that I loved God and lived with integrity. It could have happened to any man or woman. It could have happened to you.

But it happened to me. It struck without warning, like a monster from within just waiting to reveal itself. The demon picked me up gently, only to throw me down and leave me wondering what had become of my former self. All that remained was the shell of a man with a portion of his brain turned to ashes.

An event of this magnitude causes us to reevaluate life's complexities and our most cherished priorities while on earth. I have spent much time examining my fundamental values and have discovered tremendous innate value in life itself. Chances are, if you are reading this, you have been touched by stroke, and have asked similar questions.

Lots of books have been written about stroke; this book is about what stroke means to the people affected by it—and how to move on. After the stroke, I was not able to do everything I thought gave my life value before, but at the most basic level, I still had the ability to choose my response to what would become painful trials. To achieve meaningful goals, to impact the lives of others, to love—these are the things of infinite value. This realization carried me through those early days and nights immediately after the stroke. Lying still in a hospital bed, I was unable to move, have normal skin sensation, speak, or think in words. To search out and create meaning in my *new* life became my goal.

In this book, you will gain insight into the world of stroke—its causes, and how to overcome its devastating effects. You will learn the vast potential for recovery of functional abilities though, try as we may, full recovery or "going back to the way you did things before" is usually not possible. Healing is not the same thing as a cure, which most people long for. Healing involves an emotional reweaving of our life story to incorporate, not merely remove, our injuries. It involves growth and personal change, maturation into a new state despite, not in the absence of, suffering. It includes acceptance of our lost innocence, while reaching for greater wisdom. Nonetheless, through struggle, work, time, and guidance, a significant amount of function can be regained. Additionally, successful adaptations can be made for those things that do not, or cannot, come back. This is the model for life in general. Sometimes people benefit from guidance and support—someone to take you by the hand and show you the way. Eventually, the pieces of your life begin to make sense—how they fit together, how your struggles force you to grow. Your life becomes as a vibrant tree, still growing, though scarred by stroke, making room for new life, new hope, and eventual peace (as the cover to this book suggests).

Starting over from scratch is not easy, for any of us. It wasn't easy for me. But through it all, I have found that the struggle to *rise* from the ashes the stroke left in its wake has given more meaning to my life. When we overcome the trials and travails of this life, it transforms our daily and often trite challenges, and infuses them with significance. As is the case with most things, improvement comes bit by bit, piece by piece, and not in immense, categorical change, all at once. But, with time, and a lot of work, significant change does occur.

This book was born out of my extensive study of the psychology of loss and change—exploring the human condition—tempered by my own experience as a patient going through hard things, and as a stroke rehabilitation doctor who witnesses small and large triumphs on a daily basis. The challenge for most of us is finding the courage to make that first step, put one foot in front of the other, repeat, be very persistent, and then endure to the end. So it was with me, when all seemed to be lost.

I am not under the illusion that challenges and disappointments are unique to me. A large part of our experience as humans is dealing with pain and suffering. However, within each of us is the ability to find courage, strength, and purpose in our challenges and thereby transform our catastrophic defeats into victories. My goal in this book is to infuse you with enthusiasm. Every person's situation is different and unique, but this book will help identify the factors that lead to a better quality of life after stroke, including improving emotional wellbeing so you can maximize your neurologic functions and reach untapped potential. This is the time to take your life back. To do so, you will need to surround yourself with great support. This book outlines many of the steps to rebuild a meaningful life.

However, just as each person is different, each stroke is unique. A one-size-fits-all solution for stroke rehabilitation and recovery does not exist. Therefore, my purpose is to outline the concepts that form guidelines for you to use in various situations. A stroke, for most of us, will represent the greatest challenge we will ever face. But stroke is not the only challenge we will face. The ideas contained in this book will hopefully become a guide for your life. As you adapt to a new life-situation, have courage—you will be able to reach your individual life potential, whatever that may be. This book will teach you how to get into an adaptive spiral, making slow and steady progress in your resilient and irrepressible life.

Today, years after my stroke, in my role as a physician specializing in rehabilitation medicine, I come into daily contact with people who have experienced major, life-changing, catastrophic events. The patients and their families' responses are always unique and special. Some people will have a great prognosis, or potential for recovery, but carry a hopeless outlook. Others will have a bleak prognosis, but will be filled with hope. In each instance, much uncertainty exists and many questions have no simple answers. Every time I meet a new patient, I wonder what their story will be and how they will deal with the firestorm in their lives—I try to provide gentle nudges to help them see their potential, to suggest there is meaning in the suffering they now feel.

Many years after my own stroke, I was called to see a young man who had had a stroke only days before. I read his chart in preparation and then proceeded to his room. Intellectually, this was an interesting case, but, as usual, it wasn't until I met the patient that the fascinating picture of an individual life began to unfold. On the other side of the door lay a forty-six-year-old man, who, just days before, seemed to have everything going his way: married, with three great teenaged kids, a great job as a banker, and a comfortable home in the suburbs. All this came crashing down. What I saw on the other side of that door was a man stripped of his speech, paralyzed and numb on the entire right side of his body, and robbed of his dignity. His stroke had been remarkably similar to mine.

Although the man had good comprehension, he was mute and had no way to use his dominant right hand to write. I immediately recognized all he had lost. It was a quite visceral appreciation of the heights from which he had fallen—by a doctor who had not only seen this before, but had actually been there before. His story was my story.

He was alone in his room. I sat down and had a heart-to-heart talk with him. He seemed to be surprised that, though he couldn't utter a single word, nor produce any sound, I recognized he could still understand. Moreover, we recognized together that, of course, he was still human, even with the discomfort of his mortality being exposed like he had never experienced before. People universally desire to be respected, to be loved, whether they have had a stroke or not; we all live with these universal truths and desires.

As we sat, I recounted how I had been in his position. Therefore, I knew there was hope, and we would guide him for as long as it took. And although life would probably never be exactly the same, he had a chance for a meaningful, full, high quality of life again. But there was hard work ahead; I knew the challenges that lay before him. He would have to fight to regain his former abilities and life-station. I suggested that, perhaps, trials bring strength that can happen in no other way.

As I left the room, I told the man, "We will get through this together." Even though I was unsure what his outcome would be—he would likely have lifelong impairments—I also knew I was acting as a mirror, reflecting for good or for bad what he might become. I believe that sometimes a person needs a story, an example, someone to give hope, more than anything else, just to stay alive. Stories have tremendous power over the human mind, and sometimes patients need my story, more than my medical care, to help alleviate their suffering. I feel a solemn responsibility to share it, when possible. A couple of weeks later, using an assistive technology speaking device, he typed, and then the computer spoke, "I appreciate your example." Now, though it took several months, he is speaking in complete sentences. I am thrilled whenever I am able to have a conversation with him.

I am writing this book because I feel a tug to express the things most important to me, and I hope others will be able to draw understanding and strength from my insights and experience, for I know struggles are universal to the human experience. Perhaps my experience is not at all unique, but speaks to broad and basic truths that apply to each one of us.

I also know recovering from a stroke is a daunting task, and possibly a task that will take one's whole life to achieve. But through this process, one can come out of a very dark place and into the light. People can regain the quality of life they seek, albeit in ways they currently have a difficult time seeing.

A specific analogy gave me comfort in the face of all the loss my stroke caused at such a vibrant age. The metaphor is this: In a forest, the destruction from a fire and its ash makes way for new growth and new life. Since my fire, my life has been an open meadow with the potential for greater achievement, joy, and love. These fires allow rejuvenation, and more than that, a new start offers opportunities for new triumph. I want to offer some guidance to stroke survivors, caregivers, family members, and loved ones. The only question that remains is: Are you ready?

CHAPTER 1

THE CRISIS THAT WOULD DEFINE MY LIFE

Afflictions come to us all, not to make us sad, but sober; not to make us sorry, but to make us wise; not to make us despondent, but by its darkness to refresh us as the night refreshes the day; not to make us impoverished, but to enrich us.

— Henry Ward Beecher

Hard things happen in life. Hard things are a part of life. Accidents, illnesses, and injury, in spite of our best efforts, are impossible to avoid for yourself and the people you love. Bodies sometimes break down, often at inopportune times. But sometimes you've got to concede the battle so you can ultimately win the war.

Stroke is one of those many hard things in life. Stroke is one of the most intimate injuries a person can experience because stroke occurs in the brain and affects the mind. It changes your view of yourself, as well as your ability to function in the world. As you struggle to regain your life, reinvention of significant aspects of your life is often necessary—both of what you think of yourself and of how you can adapt to engage with the world once again.

This book includes the story of one doctor's stroke, and my journey back. But my experience is not unlike other stories of stroke or other serious medical problems…and the roads to recovery are also similar. That path is littered with large and small decision points that, if done right, will recreate a life that's actually worth living. But we have to get through the day-to-day tedium and be particularly persistent, while focusing on a bigger picture. Challenges and disappointments are a large part of our experience of being human, which includes dealing with pain and suffering. However, if we focus on quality of life as an ultimate end, we will be more successful in creating strategies to maximize our potential, which should be the underlying goal in all of our lives.

My own stroke was a devastating injury for me and my family. It came at a time when I was preparing to make a contribution to society through medicine, when I was working hard, gaining steam, and planning for a bright future, which now seemed to be crushed by a stroke. It was 2001, and I was riding high—I had just completed medical school at Loyola University in Chicago. I was a medical resident in Chicago, and the future looked bright for me and my young family. But in one instant, all of that changed. My future became very uncertain because of a stroke at the age of twenty-eight.

A stroke affects the entire family unit. It is hard to predict what the response from other family members will be in seeing their loved one fall from his or her white horse. Always, stroke creates tremendous strain on all involved in the social dynamic system that surrounds the stroke patient.

However, within each of us is the ability to find purpose in our challenges, and thereby turn our most catastrophic defeats and the aspects of the sting of defeat into victories. I have seen these types of stories play out, time and time again, in my work with stroke patients as the director of the stroke rehabilitation program at the University of Utah. This is not so much my story, but rather our collective story.

I have found that within each of us lies tremendous untapped potential, just waiting for the right time, the right stimulus to manifest itself. We, as individuals, hold the key. In the end, we will find that quality of life has a lot less to do with status or possessions, or even talents, and a lot more to do with our capacity to form meaningful relationships and connections with others.

I am one man among many who has experienced a stroke…and at a young age. My life before the stroke was fairly uneventful.

Struck Down

It happened on a Friday. My wife Emi and I were happy, and sometimes exhausted, to be halfway through the medical training journey, while raising our precious baby girl, Ella. We chose to stay in Chicago for one more year while I did my internship training and then planned to complete my medical residency in St. Louis.

Then, it happened out of the blue, on one unseasonably warm but otherwise routine day in early December. While getting ready for work, quite suddenly the power to speak and move on one side of my body completely left me.

I lay down on the bed on my back. When Emi asked if something was wrong, I tried to speak, but no words came out of my mouth. I tried again. Again, the content of my thoughts was present, but I was losing control of my tongue and lips. Again, I tried, this time more forcefully. A strange gurgling sound came from deep inside my throat. My heart began racing. It was like a nightmare where you have to scream out, but your voice has gone mute. Something so basic as voice and speech was being stripped from me. I tried to sit up, but by then my entire right side was limp and numb; I didn't have the strength. I was being defeated by some bizarre internal force. I had no power. Confused by the inexplicable and sudden symptoms coming over me, like nothing I had experienced before, I was unprepared, powerless, and afraid—was this what it felt like to die?

Emi quickly realized, in a moment of pure inspiration, what was going on, and called 911. I, on the other hand, had the strong urge not to jump to conclusions, wait a few moments, and figure things out, as I had been medically trained to do. Thankfully, however, the wheels were already rolling in Emi's mind; I heard Emi say in a firm, though pressured, voice to the emergency dispatcher, "My husband is twenty-eight years old, and he's having a stroke."

I was realizing that any effort to get up or move was futile. I listened to one side of the conversation between my wife and the emergency response operator.

"Yes, he seems to be breathing."

"Just a minute, let me check." Emi felt my neck for a pulse.

"Steve, can you lift your arm?" I didn't know how to respond. I knew she was asking me a question, but I didn't know what to do with the information. I couldn't lift my arm, but I was not capable of saying, "No, I can't." I was also not able to think to shake my head. Instead, I just lay there feeling brainless; somehow, my brain became disconnected from my mouth and my right side.

In a few minutes, a policeman barged into the bedroom. A couple of minutes later, more people arrived and the whole room was filled with a flurry of activity. Paramedics asking me questions for which I had no response. A penlight shining into my eyes. Paramedics tapping for reflexes. Someone calling out for the stretcher. Soon I was wheeled out the front door. The warm rays of sunshine surprised me—was this to be the final time I would feel the sun on my face, or was it a gentle reminder that my life was no longer my own? Nevertheless, this was very brief, a sliver of a reprieve from the critical situation I was in.

I was loaded into the ambulance and rushed to the local ER in a semi-conscious state. My shirt was cut from my chest, and multiple EKG leads were attached. Then, in the ambulance, I overheard talk of a massive stroke. It sunk in at that moment. What I had perceived throughout my medical training as the worst thing that could happen to a person was, in fact, at that very moment, happening to me. Fear and internal agitation boiled over; waves of nausea came over me as the psychological stress of the situation hit me. Was this worse than death? I vomited profusely in the ambulance, which made the ambulance stop and caused my internal agitation and fear to be even greater, for I knew my one and only chance was getting to the ER and receiving an invaluable clot-busting medication. I knew time was of the essence in stroke care: time is literally brain loss.

Soon after arriving in the ER, Emi was told my symptoms were strongly suggestive of a stroke caused by a blood clot in an artery in my brain. The decision was made to administer a medication called tPA, a clot-busting drug that had been shown to help resolve strokes when administered early after the onset of symptoms. I knew from my medical training that about 20 percent of stroke patients have immediate resolution of their symptoms after tPA is administered. I knew I was still within the three-hour window from stroke symptom onset, three-hours when tPA was still an option; past that point, based on the best information available in 2001, irreversible brain damage would have already occurred and the risks of giving tPA would be too great. I had been taught that giving tPA was the most important thing in acute stroke management. But, in the crisis state I was in, lapsing in and out of consciousness, all my medical knowledge was useless. I was at the mercy of the physical limitations of my body and the decisions of those around me. Emi made the right decision for me—the nurse hung the IV bag that contained the tPA and we all waited.

Although I wasn't aware of it at the time, for most people, the benefits of tPA are best seen a few *months* after the stroke. There was a lot of disappointment as the minutes passed, then turned into a couple of hours, and still we saw no improvement. At one point, a well-intentioned nurse in the ER said to me, "I'm just going to set these intubation supplies on your bed (he placed it across my chest), just in case—we don't want you to become agitated or try to get up, or anything." That was my cue just to be still and relax, not to become animated, and not even to try to sit up, with no means of communication—I felt like a 6' 5" hemiplegic weakened gorilla. The threat of being intubated and sedated, possibly for a few days, was very real in my mind.

When a nurse said, "Now, we're going to move on upstairs to the Intensive Care Unit," I was in the depths of despair and disappointment. Being admitted to the ICU, in my mind, meant the tPA didn't work. It meant I wasn't going to sleep in my own bed that night. It meant this nightmare would continue…and all I could do was wait.

Eventually, after a few hours, I found myself alone. Emi had gone to retrieve our infant daughter, Ella. I could imagine Emi cradling her, both mother and baby receiving comfort, as Emi tried to wrap her head around what had just happened and the implications for our young family.

As I lapsed in and out of wakefulness and alertness, I remember visitors swimming in and out of my field of vision. My two cousins who lived in Chicago arrived, trying to assess my consciousness by asking "yes" or "no" questions like, "Is your name Steve?," all to no avail. I was awake and alert, but I had no way, even nodding or shaking my head, of answering these simple questions. Later in the evening, my parents arrived from Salt Lake City. I felt ashamed to have my mom see me in this state. That first night, my father stayed by my side, keeping watch in the ICU.

In the immediate days after, I would try in vain to figure out what had happened to my body and to my life. Though I was conscious, I had absolutely no physical control over any aspect of my present situation.

I felt no physical pain, but there was a silent intensity to my suffering. It was much like a flash fire in my brain had instantly destroyed all I had been working for. I couldn't utter a single word; I could barely move;

I couldn't write. Yet I could feel the weight of the emotions, the loss of potential, and the loss of my ability to support my young family—slipping through my fingers.

I had a long time to think in silence, the first five days in an ICU bed, then on the medicine floor for another week, surrounded by people but very detached from the outside world because of a massive communication barrier. After a few days, I still had no way to communicate other than nodding and shaking my head. I had no idea if this situation was what it would be like for the rest of my life. Imagine being unable to participate in any conversation, even when people are talking directly to you. That was my reality, and I imagined it continuing, day after day…for an entire lifetime.

My mind was filled with confusion, confusion directed toward not knowing the next steps to get out of this situation. My medical career seemed like it was over. I had worked so very hard, only to come up short at the final buzzer. I had been planning to take care of people, to heal people; now I was the one needing care—on the other side of that juggernaut we call medicine. And not the usual, brief care for a person to get back on their feet after a broken bone or a week of the flu. I was facing the possibility of needing lifelong care. Who would provide this care? My wife? My aging parents? In-home nurses and doctors? This was my reality. To figure out the next steps became my and my family's immediate and urgent objective.

Summary

Similar to hard experiences many people have, my stroke was a difficult and life-changing event. The emotional and physical toll of stroke on individuals and families cannot be overemphasized. Like other major life events, a stroke has long-term consequences. Figuring out where to go from there became my primary challenge.

CHAPTER 2

SILENCE

If you can dream—and not make dreams your master;
If you can think—and not make thoughts your aim;
If you can meet with Triumph and Disaster
And treat those two impostors just the same;
If you can bear to hear the truth you've spoken
Twisted by knaves to make a trap for fools,
Or watch the things you gave your life to, broken,
And stoop and build 'em up with worn-out tools:
…yours is the earth and everything that's in it….

— Rudyard Kipling, "If" (excerpt)

In the days after the stroke, while I lay in the ICU and then on the neurology floor, streams of well-wishers came to visit me. Though they were always upbeat and cheerful toward me, I could occasionally sense the horror they felt at my situation—tear-stained cheeks and pitying glances gave them away. What's more, because of my profound language impairments, I was rendered mute and unable to communicate with anyone at all. This lack of communication was perhaps the most frustrating part of my experience.

During these weeks of silence, two dear friends who were Catholic Jesuit priests from Loyola Medical School came to visit me in the hospital. They explained to me that, in their tradition, sometimes they took a *vow of silence*.

Their tradition dates back several centuries to St. Ignatius of Loyola, a fifteenth-century Spanish knight. He was gravely injured in battle, and after his prolonged recovery, he "took himself to the university," believing he must first conquer himself, conquer his own mind, before trying to influence others.[1] St. Ignatius founded the Society of Jesus, whose members are called Jesuits. The vow of silence is an important part of their tradition. The Jesuits also have a focus on education and have established some of the finest universities in the world.

These Jesuits, my friends, were not some obscure people in a far-off land; they were people I had come to love and respect. They didn't explain why they occasionally took this vow; they only explained that its purpose was not to deny yourself from talking, but to be "silent before God." To listen. So I did. Unable to communicate with those around me, I vowed within myself to listen and to turn this imposed silence into something better. The Jesuit tradition of the vow of silence helped me accept my current situation and learn that some people actually choose this way of life. This became a rare opportunity.

Still, the *ability* to speak had completely escaped me, and it would evade me still for many weeks. How frustrating it was to be unable to relay my feelings to my family. After many days of being alone with my thoughts in my mute state, at a time when I was obviously in need of good communication, I yearned to have that connection through speech. I eventually figured out how to write "I love you" to my wife, Emi. With this simple phrase, written to the one who meant the most to me, the communication gap, which had been wide as the ocean, started to become a little narrower, even though we sat side-by-side on the same hospital bed. With emotions and tears flowing, we were one step closer together—language is the great connector of hearts.

As my ability to generate very simple written phrases gradually returned, I wrote down what I had been yearning to express. Simply, "I am OK," okay with my life, okay with my fate. Communication became possible, but it was still like trying to communicate through a string-and-can telephone over a wide abyss.

Psychological and Emotional Toll

I had been a student of the workings of the mind since my undergraduate education in psychology. As such, I had been introduced to the Kübler-Ross model, otherwise known as the five stages of grief. This model is helpful because it postulates a progression of emotional states experienced by patients after a severe loss, such as the loss of a loved one or a terminal diagnosis.

At that time, I was going through an incredible loss. I would have to learn (or learn to apply) those concepts I had learned in the classroom setting—now in the distinctly human classroom.

I remember how my only brother, Mark, three years younger than me, came to my side the day after my stroke, flying in from Salt Lake. He was very distraught, but he hid his emotional turmoil from me. After three days, he had to go home to Utah. I heard from my parents that Mark was taking this very hard—truly devastated about my stroke—but he would return in a couple of weeks. I was determined to show him my distinct improvement.

The highly anticipated day finally arrived. I was getting some hip strength back, which allowed me to walk with assistance and a special cane with four prongs for stability. When Mark came, he walked into the room, and we hugged, but the communication barrier was still there. I showed him how I could stand up from sitting on the bed. I tried to say some words. I attempted to say, "I am glad to still be alive," but I wasn't able to make the words. We communicated through a "twenty-questions" routine, as was often necessary. At that moment, with my brother, it all became too much. As the older brother, I was supposed to be the strong one. However, roles had reversed. My tears turned into sobbing for a few long minutes, a release of the long-held emotions that had been bottled-up for some time. The dam had burst, leading to a physical response over the next couple of hours, manifesting as tremors. The tremors baffled my doctors and left me wondering what was going on—it remains a mystery since it had never happened before or since.

I know now with a high degree of certainty that my body was panicking over the recognition of how serious my situation was, how far I had fallen, and how long the road was that still lay ahead. I was, in a sense, using Mark as a barometer of how debilitating, disabling, and catastrophic this injury to my brain was. I was in the throes of mourning my loss of function, of communication, and of my life.

Moving through these five stages became an important and critical element in my being able to overcome the hurt and disappointment I was feeling and move on with my life. Kübler-Ross described these stages as denial, anger, bargaining, depression, and acceptance. (I will explore these stages further in Chapter 18.) I experienced all five. My Jesuit friends helped me move past the first four stages and on to *acceptance.*

Silence helped me make sense of my new world. Silence gave me time to think and to process. Silence brought new hope.

The Ability to Think

I had read Edward de Bono's *The Six Thinking Hats* just a few months before the stroke; this wonderful book outlines methods of systematically looking at a situation from multiple perspectives. De Bono explains that "hats" represent different angles to view many problems. These angles include looking at the big picture, teasing out the facts, recognizing intuitive emotional feelings, using cautious and conservative logic, identifying optimistic benefits, and provoking creativity. "Thinking is the ultimate human resource," de Bono explains, so we should be focused more on explorations—"looking for what *can be* rather than what *is.*"[2] I was beginning to agree with his sentiments since this outlook was the only perspective that offered any hope for my severely disabled body. Looking at my situation from all possible angles helped me figure out a pathway in this new world, a world of new possibilities. I was constructing the mental before the physical recreation of my life. Silent thinking was all I had. My inability to speak was a mixed blessing because all I could do was think in silence, which led to my ability to plan my response.

I spent a great deal of time thinking about important questions about my life, my children, my purpose, and my plans for the future. Thinking in silence gave me the opportunity to envision my life, seeing all the different possibilities and pathways. I could choose which path I wanted to work toward. What if that small spark could lead to an explosion, a "big bang," leading to the possibility of life evolving, leading to the possibility of me getting my life back? I was looking at things from all perspectives. I was trying to make sense of the stroke and so much more. Could the act of thinking in silence allow me to conquer my own mind and gain the courage, strength, and foresight to improve my dire situation and help me have a meaningful life?

A Role for Human Spirituality

As a man of faith, but also of science, I found myself thinking about our relationship with God in the context of the laws of nature, the human body, and my medical training. I believe that not only can I be both a man of faith and a man of science, but that it is only in exploring the mysteries of faith and science that one can be a truly authentic human being—able to digest truth in all its forms, able to comprehend how all truth is compounded into one complete whole.

I looked back to my own education, secular, medical, and spiritual. I knew about the laws of nature and also about the nature of our wonderful, but very human, bodies. In my medical training, I had found it important to have a keen sense of the human body's fragility.

Just a few years before, as I studied to gain this understanding, I also realized it was important to keep myself emotionally detached from the cadavers I studied in order to cope with the uneasiness that accompanies working with the body. It wasn't long before I started to see cadavers not as once living, breathing humans, but as a pathology to be studied. As such, I allowed myself to intellectually devour this part of my training.

But I also knew my body was subject to the same natural laws as each cadaver and patient I studied. I cannot detach myself from the small, but substantial and unique, knowledge of the workings of the body, brain, and mind. Our bodies and minds are not perfect and are subject to injury, illness, and death when we fall from ladders, when the regulatory systems in our cells malfunction, causing cancerous tumors, or when any other natural laws or forces act upon them.

An injury to the brain, such as occurs with stroke, can damage many functions we consider unique to humans. The brain controls all personality, memory, reason, and judgment. Often with a stroke, damage to a portion of the brain happens silently, with little or no outward signs of injury or distress. Historically, this lack of distress understandably caused people to assume the damage caused by a stroke was God's doing or God's will. They, like us today, sometimes wondered about these seemingly senseless calamities that befall the innocent. Strokes affect the old, the young, men, women, sinners, and saints; almost 800,000 people per year suffer strokes in the United States alone.

Rabbi Harold Kushner, in his book *When Bad Things Happen to Good People*, offered this valuable insight: When God agreed to grant us the opportunity for this mortal life, perhaps He relinquished some of His power to enable us to act and *choose* for ourselves. Kushner says, "Our misfortunes are none of His doing, and so we can turn to Him for help…not to be judged or forgiven, but to be strengthened and comforted." He goes on to say, "We can be angry at what has happened to us, without feeling that we are angry at God…. Instead of feeling that we are opposed to God, we can feel that our indignation is *God's* anger at unfairness working through us, that when we cry out, we are still on

God's side, and *He* is still on ours.³"

I decided to do as Albert Einstein suggested when he said, "There are only two ways to live your life. One is as though nothing is a miracle. The other is as though everything is."[4] The way the planets and the earth orbit and the way our own bodies work and can be healed—these are absolute miracles we can see every day.

As my language skills returned to me, though I was still mute, I was able to begin writing with my left hand. To my delight, the words to a poem I had learned as a ten-year-old boy came back to me. I laboriously wrote out these lines from Robert Frost's poem, "Stopping by Woods on a Snowy Evening," for I was living in solitude and isolation because of the communication barriers, but I knew I must fight my way back to a world with other people and obligations.

> The woods are lovely, dark and deep.
> But I have promises to keep,
> And miles to go before I sleep,
> And miles to go before I sleep.[5]

Those words resonated with me then, and they resonate with me now. I recognized that I had miles to go to recover my lost abilities, and I promised myself I would.

Summary

The ability to ponder in silence allowed me to plan my response to my difficult situation and to think of different possibilities for my life. It was important to me to know that this stroke was not some supernatural punishment, but that difficult things of varying degrees happen in all our lives. I chose the optimistic way; I chose to fight quietly to get my life back.

CHAPTER 3

DOING THE HARD THINGS AND RISING

How shall there be redemption and resurrection unless there has been a great sorrow? And isn't the struggle and rising the real work in our lives?

— Mary Oliver

Echoes from History

On September 12, 1962, President John F. Kennedy gave his famous inspirational speech, attempting to rouse a nation to accomplish a seemingly impossible task, "We choose to go to the moon in this decade, and *to do the other hard things* [emphasis added], not because they are easy, but because they are *hard* [emphasis added], because that goal will serve to organize and measure the best of our energies and skills. Because that challenge is one that we are willing to accept."[1]

Almost forty years later, in another time of deep resolve in our nation, the season after 9/11, my stroke occurred. At that time, the whole world seemed to be changing. The nation was shrouded in an air of suspicion, and our nation's sense of security and safety had been threatened. President George W. Bush gave an equally inspiring speech in which he said that "[T]error attacks can shake the foundations of our biggest buildings, but they cannot touch the foundation of America… And I pray [that we will] be comforted by a Power greater than any of us, spoken through the ages in Psalms 23, 'Even though I walk through the valley of the shadow of death, I fear no evil, for You are with me.'"[2]

My stroke, my biggest challenge, occurred on the sixtieth anniversary of the attack on Pearl Harbor, "a day that will live in infamy" for our nation and for me personally. Recovery from that stroke, I soon realized, was going to be equally as daunting as going to the moon, and as frightening as 9/11. Yet it could be overcome with courage. However, in my case, it was not a nation's task; it was my personal task to overcome. My wife and I took on the task to do the hard things required—resolving to have the fortitude that would surely be necessary, and the faith and courage that our efforts would not be in vain. Recovering and living with whatever challenges arose, which would include physical, emotional, and spiritual recovery, became necessary as a fundamental shift in our thinking began to occur. The hard work of recovery would take teamwork, cooperation, and a division of labor—persistently, and over a lifetime.

However, we had to take things one day at a time, as is most often the case. Initially, I lay for hours upon hours in my ICU bed not able to do much of anything. My doctors ran various tests and scans on me, the same tests I would have been administering and observing had these been typical days in my medical training. This was typical of life in the ICU, but now I was on the other side of the curtain.

Upon seeing my MRI brain scans for the first time, I noticed big white blemishes or patches over the primary language center and the muscle control "strip" that controls the body's entire right side. I knew what those patches meant—everything I valued in my once healthy body was damaged. I was literally seeing my own demise. I fully comprehended it. In my ICU bed, I briefly had visualization, through MRI images on retinas that still functioned, projected to a brain with neurons still firing, of what my life possibilities could entail. I was facing an uncertain future with partial brain loss.

At that moment, I knew living would be the harder option. Dying may have actually been much easier. On the one hand, I could wait until my corpse-like body perished, even though it might take decades, and for decay to overtake my body in a never-ending downward spiral. Or I could work through the seemingly impossible challenges that awaited me, to reobtain my life and my livelihood. I chose to do the hard things. I chose to live. I was grateful to have this choice, and confident enough in myself and in God's assistance to heal my broken body. I was determined to continue living.

My dictum became reclaiming what was lost, and if something couldn't be reclaimed, to adapt to whatever situation was necessary. I realized this reclamation would have to be a very deliberate process. I also realized I would have to muster up the courage and fortitude to figure out what needed to be done and then execute the strategies that would lead to the achievement of that plan. While in the hospital, including the two weeks in the ICU and on the medical floor and the six weeks I spent as an inpatient on the Rehabilitation Unit, I was guided by health professionals through the recovery process. I was eventually discharged from the inpatient setting and was glad to be home with my wife and my baby girl, Ella. However, even though I was finally home, so much had changed in the last two months—my physical abilities, my language capabilities, and my outlook on life had been significantly altered. The adjustment was made a little easier the more I was able to dive into therapeutic tasks to help me be more functional in the world around me.

I began going to outpatient therapy on a daily basis. I had an arrangement worked out where I received three sessions of formal therapy each weekday and then was able to use the equipment in the outpatient therapy gym for a few hours to get additional practice. I worked on speech and language, arm and hand function, walking, gait mechanics, trotting, pool therapy, jumping, and eventually jogging. Therapy became my full-time job for several months; it also felt more natural because the outpatient therapy was at Resurrection Hospital, where I was a former medical intern. It often took a sense of purpose and resiliency to keep going without the constant formal guidance and structure of the rehabilitation team around me. Even so, it remained difficult to avoid discouragement. But I knew I had to be persistent and relentless in the pursuit of the goals I had set for myself after my stroke.

A big communication barrier still existed between me and everyone else; this barrier was especially heartbreaking between Emi and me. During this time, I came to understand more about language, first from the *lack* of language, then from the struggle for basic communication, and then finally, from the often profound difficulty of interpersonal connection through language. I also realized this last element, the difficulty with interpersonal connection, exists whether you have a language impairment or not; every one of us must work on interpersonal relationships for our entire life.

I felt an urgency to regain speech and communication as I worked intently in outpatient speech therapy. It was necessary for me to go back to the most basic building blocks of verbal communication: single syllables. Forming the lips, tongue, and vocal cords to produce the simple sounds, like "ma," and being able to differentiate this sound from the vocal-cord-induced sound of "pa," was a difficult and eye-opening experience. I relearned and practiced all the basic sounds in the English language. Soon, single sounds turned into multi-syllable words I practiced through halting conversations with therapists, family members, and friends. I enhanced the vocabulary of words I could form by reading children's books aloud, then graduated on to more age-appropriate reading.

Through all of this effort, I gained a deep appreciation that the physical universe, human emotion, and passion intersects in *language*; to love language is to love this intersection.

Only when I had language stripped from me could I fully appreciate and understand this concept. Indeed, the loss of language was the most frustrating aspect of having a left-brain stroke. It is strange to be talking normally one minute and the next to be unable to operate your tongue and scarcely able to phonate. But being stripped of many faculties I had previously taken for granted, particularly language, and having to fight a battle raging on in my own mind and brain was perhaps the only way to learn important lessons through experience. These lessons can be summarized in two general categories: 1) The brain's ability to significantly recover through the persistent and deliberate work of therapy, and 2) The mind's ability to figure out successful strategies to adapt, if there is motivation to do so.

Neurologic Restoration and Adaptations

My persistent struggle with language and communication most aptly illustrates the brain's ability either to restore function or to learn strategies to adapt. Even simple writing was difficult and challenging. The first time I tried to write on the computer keyboard, I wrote, "Steve reads books about mountains," and it took me half an hour. The letters were so foreign to me. I have come to appreciate that letters and words are really just symbols we use to translate thoughts into something we can communicate to others—sometimes with simplicity, sometimes with great elegance, and yet other times with great subtlety. The reason I referred to myself in the third person in that first typed sentence says a lot about the role I was in after my stroke vs. my previous role of successful medical resident and steady father which I so badly longed to return to. I see now that I had a hard time accepting that this was now who I was.

Eight weeks later, typing words had become easier because I had relearned the keyboard's essentials. However, my typing required me to learn a one-handed technique. Through persistent and deliberate effort, I regained significant language skills, but I still needed to figure out a strategy to adapt for my right hand. (Today, I still use a one-handed typing technique—to write full-length books).

As far as spoken language, early in the recovery process, I tried all manner of things—reading aloud, singing, saying nursery rhymes, attempting to sing karaoke—all in an effort to get my brain circuitry working again.

With time, although my speech remained halting and labored, I gained the ability to speak with others, even holding some simple conversation. I realized, however, that to be an active member of society, and an effective doctor, public speaking was necessary, at least occasionally.

Putting Strategies into Practice

I was asked to speak to a congregation at a local church just six months after the stroke. As emotionally challenging as this was, I knew I had to do it. I felt I needed to do it, and in a sense, I wanted to do it. I knew doing so would display my deficits, as if they were on exhibit, but I would swallow my pride and show my community the new "Steve Edgley," come what may—and publicly face an uncertain future.

I had learned that public speaking and language are powerful and crucial ways to connect with the rest of humanity. I needed that form of connection to be part of my future. The walk up to the pulpit was short. I began speaking, one word at a time, with awkward deliberateness.

Afterward, I still felt uneasy about exposing myself. However, I knew it was an important step toward the things I wanted to do and the person I wanted to be. Nonetheless, it took courage to do this small and seemingly insignificant thing and to take many more small steps throughout my recovery process.

Just a few years after speaking to the church congregation, I was invited to speak at my first national medical conference in Park City, Utah. My topic was emerging techniques in stroke rehabilitation. I had certainly come a long way in my speaking ability in those long years, but my speaking was far from perfect and something I was very timid—even embarrassed—about. After approaching the pulpit and doing the obligatory A/V microphone check, "Can you hear me in the back?" a man called out, "We can hear you; we just can't understand you!"

Jerk, I thought to myself…but then I was able to press on, dig in, and soldier through the speech. I lived to speak another day. Now, I have spoken to local and national audiences dozens of times.

Doing the hard things sometimes required ingenuity. As I worked to recover, I thought a lot about the space missions, including overcoming disaster in the space program. I contemplated the Apollo 13 mission, launched in April 11, 1970, only to be aborted due to an oxygen tank explosion. Getting the three astronauts safely back to earth required heroic and masterful planning and execution. Miraculously, through the efforts of many bright and talented people, the adaptation strategies were successful and the astronauts were able to splash down in a totally different ocean on the other side of the earth.

I was hoping for a similar miracle—not to get me back to earth, but to find a way back to being a productive member of society—and I even had hopes of getting back into the field of medicine and to a semblance of my former life. Much like the NASA engineers and astrophysicists, I needed to assess the situation, be creative, figure out what tools and resources I still possessed, and maximize usage of those tools and resources. Climbing a mountain is a process of taking one small step, and then another, and another. Creatively figuring out the appropriate next steps and then actually *doing* them is usually our challenge. I could not panic or quit; I had to work steadily and with purpose. Such was my mission. I realized I didn't have time or energy to wallow in self-pity. There would be mid-flight adjustments; I was sure of that. I might even need to splash down on the other side of the world like Apollo 13 had. If it would take me changing medical fields and making extensive adaptations, that's what I was going to do, for I was a new man. I *could* do this. I *would* do this.

Summary

We can learn from a history of past successes or a remembrance of past personal adversity and eventual success. When recovering from a stroke, significant recovery is possible with consistent and deliberate work and therapy. However, adaptations usually need to be made. Above all, a person's motivation and ambition level can make a tremendous difference in the overall outcome.

CHAPTER 4

CONQUERING THE MIND

Do not waste life in fears and doubts. Spend yourself on the work before you, well assured that the right performance of this hour's duties will be the best preparation for the hours or ages that follow.

— Ralph Waldo Emerson

Our doubts are traitors, and make us lose the good we oft might win by fearing to attempt.

— William Shakespeare

In his book *The Seven Habits of Highly Effective People*, Dr. Stephen R. Covey explains the concept and importance of the paradigm through which we see the world:

> Paradigm comes from the Greek word "paradigma." It basically means a pattern, a model, a representation, something that stands for something else. It comes from the mental image you have in your mind of the way things are "out there." The images we carry in our heads of the way things are, of reality, come from our own background, our own experiences.[1]

A paradigm is like a mental roadmap—what we think about ourselves and the world will, to a large extent, create our reality. When we experience something as life-altering as a stroke, it is essential to look through the best possible, self-affirming, and real paradigms.

Goal Setting

I was raised in a family and culture that valued goal setting, and after my stroke, I soon realized the most important thing I could do to enact my recovery was to set and achieve goals, both small and large. I also recognized it would be critical to have someone guide me through the process, and I was fortunate to have a good rehabilitation team. I wrote my goals in a notebook and crossed off each one when I attained it. Today, that notebook is a valuable record of my effort and my successes.

My process reminds me of a story about a boy in a toy store. The boy sees a self-righting, punching dummy. No matter how hard he hits the dummy and knocks it down, it always pops right back up. Seeing how the boy is fascinated, his dad asks, "Why do you suppose the punching bag always stands right up again?" The boy replies, "I guess he's standing up on the inside." Often, maybe most of the time, we have to dig within our own soul and character first, persistently, day after day, before we see success.

I checked off goals I had completed and wrote new goals that would stretch me. I worked hard in therapy, and the therapists began giving me more than the requisite three hours per day and more of their attention. On the weekend, I began to get in trouble when the nurses couldn't find me in my room; they learned to check the physical therapy gym first, where I could be found working my muscles on the therapy mat, doing my exercise routine. I began working on numerous things, once simple things that were now indescribably difficult. Looking back, Helen Keller's words resonated in my soul, "I cannot do everything, but I can do something. I must not fail to do the something that I can do." I was overcome with emotion the first time I showed Emi and my family how I could stand up from a sitting position. Tears flowed freely.

Later, my physical therapist and I got into a routine, working together; she knew how to guide me in the small but significant steps of recovery. One week I was walking with a walker and an ankle brace, with her assistance to steady me. The following week, I was walking with a four-pronged cane, then with a single-point cane, and then with no cane at all. I tried the Nu-Step, a type of recumbent stair-stepper, for the first time and, in my enthusiasm, overworked myself; I spent the evening with muscular tremors I couldn't control. Eventually, I was able to extend my knee, and then bend it. Later came bending my elbow, and then extending it. Each movement became a small yet significant victory I shared silently with my therapists and family. However, getting the strength back to do simple movement was just the first step. Motor control and coordination were next. Learning how to sense the position of my limbs in space became another step, and on and on in a seemingly never-ending process.

I began working with speech therapists and could eventually produce one syllable sounds, such as "ma, ma" or "pa, pa." Soon, by the time I left inpatient rehabilitation, I could write and speak in phrases, though my speech was extremely halting and hard to understand. I had an especially difficult time with the "r" sound, the way the back of the tongue has to sit just right, and the way the tongue curls at the end of the sound—things most of us just take for granted. Who knew?

I completed six weeks of vigorous inpatient rehabilitation. When I got home, I realized the real work was just beginning. I also realized I had to create a vision for myself of what I could accomplish. This stimulated a rise in my confidence and my motivation. What I envisioned for my future made a tremendous difference in what I eventually achieved. I had to develop the will to do everything within my power to recover as much function as I could. Determining what I thought I could achieve was the first step in figuring out ways to will my own brain to take steps to recovery and to adapt to the challenges placed before me.

In this period of recovery, I did many things that confused the people around me, including those closest to me. It was just so hard to explain myself in detail, including to the people who probably needed explanations the most.

Persistence

On one trip to visit my in-laws in Salt Lake City, I noticed a bucket of Brio railroad parts, a young child's toy, in their home. Still in intense therapy for my hemiparetic right arm and leg, I realized this was the therapy tool I had been looking for. For a couple of hours each day, I assumed various positions on the floor working with the toy set. Picking up the railway pieces with my right hand, supporting my weight while sitting on the floor with my right arm, and working on trunk control was very important to my recovery process, even if to the outside observer, I was merely "playing" with a child's toy. Assembling the tracks in a design was an appropriate visuospatial cognitive exercise as well. In a situation where I had a finite amount of time to regain the abilities I had lost, I was willing to do whatever it took to regain them, even if only by small increments. I had to be willing to do hard, and sometimes humiliating, things.

While on that same trip to Salt Lake City, we stopped at my boyhood home, where my parents still live, and I decided to make hard candy suckers. Making suckers was how, as a young boy of ten or eleven, I had earned money for things I wanted to buy. Now, my parents thought it quite unusual and childlike for their adult son to pull out the old sucker molds and proceed to make candy. However, for me, it was a very deliberate act. I was very interested in the challenge of remembering and following the recipe, and in physically testing myself, with only one working hand, to see if I could complete the task. It may have been somewhat humiliating, but I had to be willing to do the hard things (and in this case, the results were delicious).

About six months after my stroke, one of my therapists learned of an advanced recovery technique called constraint-induced movement therapy (CIMT). A multicenter research study was enrolling stroke patients with similar stroke characteristics to mine, and we determined the intense therapy would be good for my recovery. The idea with CIMT is to put the patient in an environment where they are required to do everything with their impaired limb (in my case, my right arm and hand). Patients are immersed in that environment, with their healthy limb restrained so they have to use the impaired limb. The main site of the study was in Birmingham, Alabama. Emi and I determined it would not be practical for her to go to assist me while caring for our one-year-old baby, Ella. Instead, my dear and patient mother was willing to come with me. We flew together and checked into the hotel where we would stay for sixteen days. I was driven to do all I could to regain function; even if this new therapy failed, I knew it was important at least to try. A large component of this form of therapy is the restraining of the good, functional arm, thereby forcing you to use your impaired arm. The concept is sound: goal-directed, task-specific, repetitive practice, eight hours per day for two weeks. I knew this type of intense therapy would be good for my recovery of hand and arm function. It was the steady, persistent, and complete immersion I felt I needed.

I did not anticipate, however, the physical and emotional toll it would take. This toll, in part, was due to being in a new setting, without my usual support, with my young family temporarily torn apart. The therapy was also grueling. My resolve was certainly tested many times throughout this experience of working hard and struggling for recovery.

At the end of this two-week, intense therapy period, my hand and arm function were marginally better; however, the progress was less than I desired. Although I relearned how to use my shoulder, elbow, and wrist more effectively, yielding great dividends in the ensuing years, my hand function did not improve nearly to the point I had hoped. I had lofty goals for my hand to regain the function needed to operate surgically as a doctor, but after this treatment, I could perform only simple grasp-and-release activities and was unable even to move my fingers independently of one another. Nevertheless, *any* improvement was welcomed and valuable to me. And although I did not improve to the point I wished, my arm and hand function did improve. This study was found to be a success for most patients, though most patients are not able to achieve 100 percent full recovery of their hand. Still, the CIMT principles that stemmed from this study form an important and valuable component of the therapy we use in the outpatient clinic where I work today.

Unfortunately, regardless of our efforts, we usually cannot make our brain tissue be completely whole again. In spite of neuroscience and plasticity (the ability of the brain to change itself), once an area of the brain is damaged, the tissue does not miraculously grow back and restore itself. Once an area of the brain becomes damaged, other parts of the brain have some capacity to make up for the damaged tissue, but this capacity is limited. While every portion of the brain is responsible for some important function, some areas are more critical to the function of the things we highly value. These highly specialized regions are called *eloquent tissue*. For example, your dominant hand and your speech center are controlled by this eloquent tissue. Almost 50 percent of all stroke patients have a loss of dexterity in their affected hands, which represents a great burden to a significant number of people. A person can often bring back some function in eloquent tissue, thereby partially regaining some function (sometimes called restoration of latent potential). However, this recovery of function, although significant, is usually incomplete.

Thus, speech will likely always be slightly halting. My right hand and arm will likely also be permanently impaired. As I attempted to reinvent myself and transition into a new beginning, I was still hoping to make a full recovery. However, as I worked through therapy and the physical aspects of recovery, it became apparent that my physical recovery would be less than complete.

Even though my recovery was tremendous and my doctors were all pleased with my remarkable progress, the physical recovery was far from complete. However, I did not anticipate the amount of adaptation that would eventually be necessary. It was a battle to conquer my own mind and to find the will to discover meaningful strategies to accommodate my new situation.

Embrace the New Person You Are Becoming

The strategies necessary to find success in adapting and accommodating are possibly the hardest aspects of healing, and possibly also the most under-appreciated because they require a degree of humility and an admittance that things will not be the way they were before the stroke. However, it is imperative that you find a new way forward. Remember that others have gone before you to find a new path. In fact, making large life adjustments may be a universal human experience. Henry David Thoreau stated, "I know of no more encouraging fact than the unquestionable ability of man to elevate his life by conscious endeavor."[2]

I realized I would have to make some major adjustments in my life and work. I was advised by my therapist to learn how to take advantage of assistive technology. Voice-to-text technology was just coming out, and I anticipated it could assist me in my goal to return to work as a resident-physician since I didn't have use of my right hand. I would need this technology to document patient histories and physicals and to write progress notes. In learning how to use assistive technology, I was trying to prepare myself for the endless medical documentation of the healthcare field. I wanted to work as efficiently as other residents rather than slowly handwrite with my left hand or type things out one-handed. As I worked with an assistive technology specialist to learn how to use a speech-to-text program, I gained confidence that I could adapt to my new situation and a busy workplace environment.

For example, to accommodate for the usual way I rested my other wrist on the paper I was writing on, I learned to secure the paper to a clipboard, complete with a calculator built in to the top of the board. This became, in a sense, a *comfort blanket* for my writing activities at work.

I spent hundreds of hours trying to regain full function of my hand, speech, and body, trying to achieve every ounce of physical recovery I could. It wasn't like a miraculous restoration of neural connections to my cells and muscles. However, I learned to recognize that I *did* progress physically, and had the capacity to adapt. Through the neurological recovery *and* by employing successful adaptations, my recovery was sufficient.

This recovery period and time of my life wasn't all doldrums and tedium, thankfully. "In life, if you're not having fun, you're not doing it right," one of my stroke patients told me years later. I decided I needed to have fun during my recovery, so I set a goal to learn to run again. I had run the Chicago Marathon and competed in a few triathlons the year prior to my stroke. Running the Chicago Marathon had been one of the most exhilarating experiences of my life, and I was eager to get back to some sort of competition. After extensive work with my physical therapists, as well as practice on my own, I was able to run effectively, though not at the competitive level of my pre-stroke days. Nevertheless, about seven months after the stroke, I signed up for a 5K race and went all out. By the race's end, I was utterly exhausted. I had a more difficult time forming words—my mind and my body were overtaxed and drained. However, it had been good for my confidence. After running this race, I thought it was at least possible to have the endurance and stamina needed to work the grueling schedule of a medical resident.

Whether we recover fully from an illness or are led down a different path than we originally planned, we have the opportunity to reach our full potential, which is defined as simply summoning up the best you have within you…nothing more. This life is full of hard things, and we can learn and grow from all of life's experiences.

Summary

When faced with challenges, your own mind can be your greatest asset, but it can also be an obstacle to overcome. Goal-setting and persistence can guide your way. However, what you think about your potential to recover function and your willingness to adapt will largely determine your success.

CHAPTER 5

WHEN A DOOR CLOSES, BUILD A NEW ONE

Do not lose heart, even if you must wait before finding the right thing, even if you must make several attempts. Be prepared for disappointment, but do not abandon your quest.

— Albert Schweitzer

Life Reimagined

It is often said, "When a door closes, a window opens." However, sometimes when that door closes, there *are* no windows, and we find ourselves in a very dark place. This is sometimes a result of the natural and imperfect world we live in, or because of maladies with our wonderful, though imperfect, bodies, such as the misfortune of stroke. At those times, the power is often within us to do some remodeling on our own life situation, to choose to improve our circumstances, and to enable us to get back to our life journey. I respect wherever you might fall on the faith and religion spectrum, and I don't believe God "causes" the misfortunes that befall us; however, this quote by C. S. Lewis offers an interesting paradigm to consider:

> Imagine yourself as a living house. God comes in to rebuild that house. At first, perhaps, you can understand what He is doing. He

is getting the drains right and stopping the leaks in the roof and so on; you knew that those jobs needed doing and so you are not surprised. But presently He starts knocking the house about in a way that hurts abominably and does not seem to make any sense. What on earth is He up to? The explanation is that He is building quite a different house from the one you thought of—throwing out a new wing here, putting on an extra floor there, running up towers, making courtyards. You thought you were being made into a decent little cottage: but He is building a palace. He intends to come and live in it Himself.[1]

With this in mind, I tried to view my own life, the new life I was trying to build, through these optics. It would require an aggressive, almost violent approach to rebuild my life from the dark desolation I felt. However, it was an act of faith and trust to know where to swing the sledge hammer and where to construct the new door.

Returning to medical residency and finally becoming a doctor was my main goal. I felt the urgency of completing my medical residency. I knew the longer I waited, the less likely I was to return to medicine. I set my goal at one year. But even after a year of extensive rehabilitation and retraining, all my confidence was still required to pursue that goal.

The Importance of Meaningful Work

It is very important to most people, stroke survivors included, to find meaningful ways to give back to the community. Whether it's returning to work or volunteering, the act of giving back facilitates your self-confidence and self-esteem. In my personal journey, because I was so young, with a lot of years ahead of me, returning to work was especially important.

For me to have a chance for success, I knew I needed to have a mass of people on my side, all with the impetus to work with me to achieve my goal of returning to medicine. Fortunately, it seemed as though I did have large scale support, from the hospital's administrative directors to fellow residents and staff. Of note, I had the support of the residency program director at Resurrection Hospital, the site of my prior intern experience. He was willing to take me back, though it was very apparent to everyone, including myself, that I still had some major hurdles to navigate. Communication was extremely difficult, with colleagues and with patients, and doing essentially everything with my non-dominant left hand was challenging, to put it mildly. However, we'd signed the residency contract, and a date to return to residency had been set for early December.

I restarted residency training as a humble and broken vessel, eager to fulfill that unspoken commitment to provide for and protect my young family—while bearing my own set of impairments for everyone to see. My journey ultimately led me to the field of stroke rehabilitation—with purpose, for I had been on both sides of the curtain, a patient who then became a doctor, and I could imagine what such a doctor would have meant to me. I did this despite my impaired right arm and hand, my speech impediment, and my partial paralysis in my right foot and ankle. These impairments and the necessary adaptions, over time, have become second nature to me. I have attempted to attain a high quality of life. This quality of life, I have found, comes primarily through family and social connectivity and relationships built from interactions at home, at work, and with friends. Returning to work was important for many reasons, but these reasons boil down to a common element: human relationships.

By making it through my intern year, I had returned to a career in medicine, a major goal achieved, but there was still more training and changes to come in our lives.

Toward the end of my intern year, I formally made a decision that would shape the remainder of my career: I chose to pursue the field of physical medicine and rehabilitation. I thought working with the brain and mind would grant me the opportunity to empathize with patients, showing compassion with both my knowledge and my experience. I interviewed at several top programs, including the Mayo Clinic, University of Washington, and University of Utah. I was eventually offered positions at all three, which meant we had a decision to make. On the one hand, the opportunity to study and work at places like the Mayo Clinic and University of Washington was prestigious and exciting. However, I felt Emi and I, both individually and as a couple, could only endure so much. We had broad family support in Salt Lake City, which, at times, was much needed, so we chose the University of Utah's young and growth-oriented program. I also chose Utah because I saw in the faculty and staff a passion for excellence in rehabilitation medicine.

I settled in to my residency, then became a full-fledged doctor and young assistant professor of medicine. Over the years, I have seen thousands of stroke patients in my medical practice. Some patients do better than I have but some, unfortunately, do worse.

Through it all, I have tried to make achieving a high quality of life a priority, and to teach other stroke patients principles of success in regaining quality of life. Later, I will outline some keys to regaining the ability to thrive after stroke—principles we all need reminding of from time to time. These principles are ways to obtain capacity and self-confidence, and then build relationships with others.

Facing challenges has become a large part of my life. Every day, I am reminded that simple things are not as easy as they were before the stroke. However, knowing the glass is still half-full, and being able to make the necessary adaptations, I have found a great life, for which I am thankful. In my youth, I had no idea what hardships might come in life, but through difficult life lessons, I now know that *because* of difficult things, we can learn and grow in character and in happiness. We are able to *choose* to make it bitter or sweet, but that is a decision we all have to make again and again throughout our lives. Here are five things, backed by scientific research, that I have found helpful.

1. **Seeing the "good" in your life:** Doing so, even just once a week, forces recognition that the glass is half-full and significantly increases one's level of happiness.[2] Daily meditation, prayer, and mindfulness exercises are effective tools to help you recognize there is good in your life and gain a greater sense of peace.
2. **Having a healthy and secure role in your family and community:** Usually, adaptations must be made after a stroke because of the shuffling of roles and responsibilities. Learn to slow down and appreciate every day. Again, adaptations will be necessary, but it is possible that relationships are sometimes *improved* after serious neurological injury.[3] Ultimately, it's up to each of us to find a role we can feel good about—one that contributes to our families and our communities.
3. **Being socially connected:** Our brains are wired to seek membership in a tribe, which keeps us happier and healthier. In a sense, deep, long-lasting friendships that aid in socialization are important to our spirits and our bodies.[4]
4. **Engaging in physical activity and exercise:** We can literally transform our brains through intentional effort, and one of the best ways is through physical activity, specifically aerobic exercise. Input from all our senses—visual, auditory, smell, skin sensation, and taste—sends a flood of pleasure that can create a virtual symphony in our minds. It's truly remarkable.[5]
5. **Finding opportunities to learn, grow, and serve others:** These things strengthen our confidence and support our connections with the people in our communities, especially if we use our energy to look outside of ourselves and serve others.[6]

Our lives are full of challenges, both large and small, but we can nourish our brain to obtain additional happiness in our lives. It has been said that life, if you are on the right track, is going to be uphill. It may not be an unbearably steep climb, but pushing ourselves to improve, adapt, grow, and serve others, even in the face of severe challenges, is one of the critical components to attaining happiness and a high quality of life.

The strength to move on in spite of challenges comes partially from our own effort, which stems from what you believe in your heart and in your mind. A person's level of confidence plays a role in their ability to persist into growth, or from lack of confidence, to give up. Exciting doors opened for Emi and me even as others closed. A quote, often misattributed to Henry David Thoreau, offers this insight, "Happiness is like a butterfly; the more you chase it, the more it will elude you, but if you turn your attention to other things, it will come and sit softly on your shoulder." Perhaps we are making a palace of our lives and guiding the things of utmost importance to us—family, education, career, and our highest aspirations—even if we are not always doing so in the ways we had expected. Looking through the optics to recognize the palace being built around us requires a long-term perspective.

Summary

Your stroke will likely lead to a fundamental change in your life. However, this change usually does not entail a fundamental change in the attributes of your character. Regaining confidence leads to increased motivation. By focusing on getting back a high quality of life and building personal relationships, you can achieve success and a more meaningful life.

CHAPTER 6

HUNTER AND PREY

> *I recall the two wolves chasing the snowshoe hare across the field. How fast they claimed that animal as their prize.... I think about this as we turn our backs on the wolves, and head deeper into the woods. I try to bury the worry, because we're not rabbits. We are humans. We are hunters. We are not prey.*
>
> — Victoria Scott, *Hear the Wolves*

The mind is the key to both reaching our individual potential and unlocking the mysteries of the cosmos; the human brain creates the lens through which we see the universe. In this sense, the human mind *is* our whole universe—individually. In knowing ourselves, we are coming to know our *brain*; in exploring science, we are also exploring our own brain.

To navigate the obstacles and barriers in stroke recovery, it is important to have knowledge about the process that leads to stroke, the various categories of strokes, and the usual features of common stroke syndromes, meaning common constellations and patterns of various stroke types. My purpose here is not to provide a comprehensive, all-inclusive discussion into all aspects of stroke and stroke recovery but rather to arm you with needed knowledge and to give you a flavor of stroke syndromes.

We can learn much from the profound experiences Victor Frankl endured at Auschwitz and the important lessons he learned there about human nature. Through his experience in a concentration camp, Frankl came to believe a person's primary source of motivation is not for pleasure, but for life to be significant and meaningful.

Mental health, according to Frankl, "is based on a certain degree of tension, the tension between what one has already achieved and what one still ought to accomplish, or the gap between what one is and what one should become."[1] Through his terrible and horrific experiences as a prisoner in the concentration camp, Frankl found that this tension can even be a matter of life and death. He writes that those within the concentration camp who had a sense of unfinished business and unquenched purpose were more likely to survive the ordeal. "A man who becomes conscious of the responsibility he bears towards a human being who affectionately waits for him, or an unfinished work, will never be able to throw away his life."[2] In a sense, Frankl survived because he was able to keep hope alive; he was able to will his mind to survive.

A spectrum exists for human response to adversity and how we choose to adapt. However, our response can be broken down into four broad categories:

- succumbing to adversity
- surviving with diminished quality of life
- being resilient (returning to baseline quality of life)
- thriving (growth)[3]

Our response and approach to coping with adversity can determine our outlook on life—for the rest of our lives.

Stroke is a terrible thing that may have happened to you or happened to someone you care about. At some point, it's important to turn the misfortune on its head and become the hunter, not the prey.

We have not been through a concentration camp, but those of us who have been touched and affected by stroke have gone through a very personal Auschwitz, one that strips us down to the bone, and although our medical and rehabilitation supporting staff may be exceptional, stroke is still a very personal trial from which we have to find our way back—physically, emotionally, and spiritually—for ourselves. Hence, it's up to each of us to choose whether to see ourself as a victim of circumstance, or to fight, crawl, and claw our way back. Everyone, whether or not they have had a stroke, has limits to their potential. After a stroke, people question their worth and, although no one can tell them what their individual potential is, they *do* have worth—always. There *is* untapped potential within every person—potential for growth and success.

The Adaptive Spiral

Individual differences in coping strategies put some people on a maladaptive spiral, whereas others proceed on an *adaptive spiral*. The adaptive spiral has been found to encompass improved interpersonal relationships, a changed or developing philosophy of life, and positive change in perception of self.[4] The adaptive spiral refers to a positive pattern of behavior from which you build the foundation of success. In this book, I define the adaptive spiral as entailing four factors, which are a modified form of the Continuum of Change as defined by Carmen Gloria de las Heras. This modified continuum of change creates the scaffolding on which the adaptive spiral can thrive. The four factors of this model are:

1. Confidence and motivation: the will to do
2. Exploration: examining the world and what you can do in it
3. Competency: developing personal capacities
4. Achievement: growth, leading to more confidence…and the cycle continues

For growth on the adaptive spiral to take place, proper understanding of what you are up against and the obstacles that exist between your current self and the self you want to become are required. Knowledge is power in helping you attain a more meaningful life.

Individual Victory

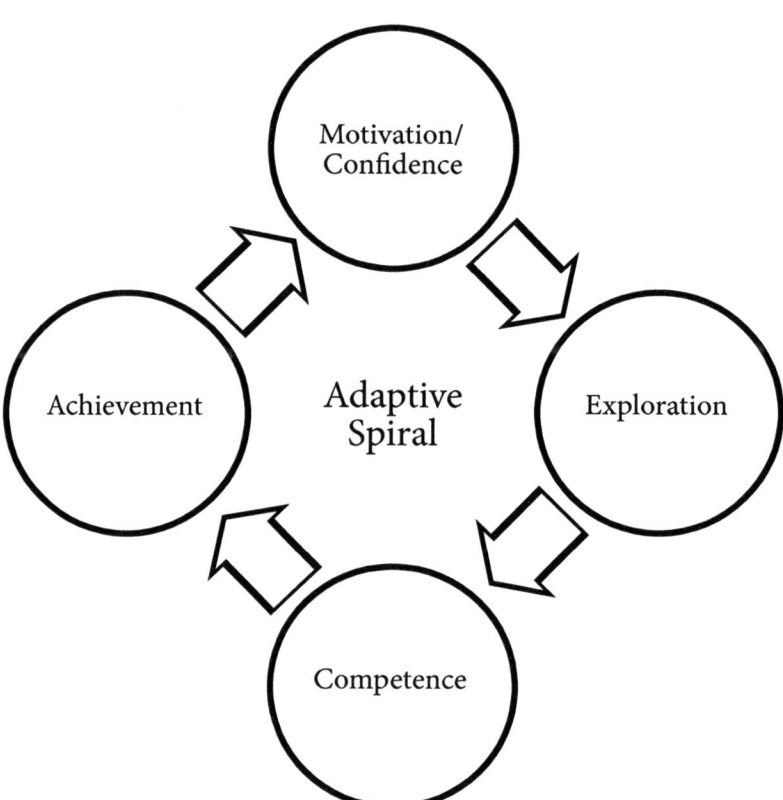

If you choose strategies that embrace the adaptive spiral, you will be equipped to continue your journey to rebuild your life in meaningful ways in an ever-upward spiral.

Mustard Seed: The Power of Confidence and Motivation

I have no memory of having an actual conversation with Grandfather Edgley. He died when I was barely nine. However, I know he was a kind, empathetic, generous man. I know this because of a gift passed along to my aunt and, eventually, to me, fifty years later.

His youngest daughter, Marcia Edgley, was just six years old in the early 1950s when she contracted a severe case of polio. Bed-bound for months, Marcia faced a future of multiple muscle reattachment surgeries and a whole lifetime of disability. She was in an iron-lung for a time. She was transferred many times between hospitals in Idaho and Utah. My grandfather was distraught for his little girl.

In his inability to perform some miracle for his precious child, at some point in a multi-year process, he gave her what may have been just as good and powerful a gift as making her whole once again. He gave her a tiny mustard seed.

The mustard seed is one of the smallest seeds of any tree. In antiquity, people marveled that this tiny seed could grow into a mighty tree. Planting that seed required foresight, faith, and care. My grandfather told his little six-year-old, bed-bound daughter that if she would believe and nurture her faith, though it was only the size of a mustard seed, she would one day do great things. He taught her that we cannot control what happened to us in our past, but we can control our future and create our own meaning and purpose in the midst of a terribly disabling lifelong condition. If she would have faith and work toward goals, she too would develop as a mighty and strong mustard tree.

By the time I met Marcia, she was in her late thirties, and, with her husband Ben, was raising three outstanding and spirited girls. She wore her impairments well, though they were obvious to everyone who watched her walk, move, or live. I thought her stair-glide, the track elevator which she rode up and down the stairs in her home, looked like fun, but it was off-limits to us kids. I noticed her legs didn't bend the same way as my seven-year-old legs, and that her feet were smaller than mine. She never complained, carrying on with quiet dignity. She also became a leader in her community and was definitely an inspiration to those who knew her.

Later, while I was in college, I was visiting the home of one of my friends, whose mother was friends with Marcia when they were both in college. She told me, with emotion, how Marcia had profoundly affected her life by her example.

Then, fifty years after the onset of Marcia's polio, I was the one bedbound from a severe stroke. I was the one who was mute and who had severe paralysis and other neurologic effects. I was the one facing a crushed future, dreams dashed, and little hope.

At that time, I received a letter from Marcia. As I opened it, the tiniest of boxes fell out, and I saw it contained a single tiny seed—a mustard seed—a gift from my grandfather to her, and now to me. The message was the same; the seed represented the potential of humans to overcome and do good. But that seed needed to be planted, requiring foresight, faith, and care. It would take belief in myself plus work for it to develop into a mighty and strong mustard tree. "He who has a why to live for can bear with almost any how," Nietzsche is credited with saying.

Exploration

About six months after my stroke, in order to nurture my mustard seed, I was doing all I could along my recovery path. I joined a gym, which was very helpful for the home exercise program my therapists had taught me. I struggled through various activities because I believed that struggle and gradually overcoming that struggle was the way muscles strengthen, and, by the same concept, brains and nerve connections get strengthened, as well.

Eventually, I gravitated toward some of the equipment and activities I used to enjoy. One day, I gathered the courage to approach a spinning class instructor at the gym. After I explained my situation in my halting speech, she reluctantly allowed me to participate in one of her non-busy classes so she could give me special attention if I needed it. We determined it would be difficult to keep my partially paralyzed foot on the pedal, so I obtained some used cycling shoes that would, in essence, lock my foot on the pedal. It was and always is a little challenging to "clip in" and lock my foot to the pedal, especially at first. I would climb on the bike, using the limits of my balance and strength. I would then attempt to click the pedal's locking mechanism, which required my foot to be in just the right position, putting just the right force through the foot at just the right angle. It was a feat of coordination and strength, which most people take for granted. I struggled with this, sometimes for 5-10 minutes. But I persisted. During the first few times I was successful in getting clipped-in, I relearned the pedaling motion quickly. I was emotional because it felt like it was the first time I was able to really use my broken body for rigorous exercise—a profound, moving, and beautiful experience for me. It became important for me to develop personal strengths and capacities in this and other activities. It was important that I first gained a sense of security in my environment—in this case, the gym. I was able to explore the function of my new body in a fun, structured way.

This experience became a pattern of trying new things—some things stuck; others, I moved on from. I learned, worked, and sweated to a whole host of activities. This pattern of confidently trying something new, even though the activities took me out of my comfort zone, created a virtuous cycle or an adaptive spiral. The adaptive spiral leads to a pattern of action or behavior where a small success in acquiring a new skill leads to more confidence, which leads to more practice, higher skill levels, and more confidence.

Competency

This fighting for a road back does not mean things will be the same as before. Life goals get altered and adjusted, but we all have to find purpose and meaning in life. To do so may make the difference in being a complete human being, even though paralyzed on one side, as many of us are. Each one of us can find new meaning, and let that new meaning be the motivating fuel we need to fill the gap between what we are *now* and what we can become. In the competency stage, we increase our self-efficacy and eventually develop a sense of responsibility. For me, as my physical capabilities came back, though only partially, my confidence in a whole host of things grew. I was eventually able to apply the things I was learning to be competent in practical elements of my home life and then my work life. Interestingly, I came to find that many of the things I had sought for earnestly—money, prestige, and power—were not as important as I had thought.

Achievement

As we persist and gain new competencies, we gain in achievements. It is important to recognize these milestone achievements, large or small, as we rebuild our autonomy, bit by bit. We can and must facilitate new challenges, while seeking resources, as needed. I certainly leaned on various therapists along the way for their expertise. I also sought help from my state's vocational rehabilitation department, which was quite valuable in providing advanced computer training to augment and assist the adaptations necessary for my return to work.

Perhaps, all human action and behavior initiates with a thought in the mind—a seed, a spark—growing into an idea, a concept, strengthened by a visual image or sometimes supported by a story, and developing into action. Perhaps this evolution and development is our purpose—and we can see glimpses of the story of our lives, with chapters still unwritten. The gestation of great character in human beings and great accomplishments in our world are in these unwritten chapters. Our lives can have meaning, even though each of our lives will invariably play out in unpredictable ways. This world is *our* forest; therefore, we can stop being the prey and begin being the hunter.

Even if you believe you no longer possess the skills or abilities required or are not prepared or powerful enough to make a difference, you can still make something extraordinary out of your life. Martin Luther King, Jr., said, "Everyone can be great because everyone can serve.... You only need a heart full of grace. A soul generated by love." In the end, evidence exists that what brings the most happiness is loving *relationships*.

Focusing on finding and pursuing a new life's purpose, cherishing the simple pleasures, and developing relationships with others will help transform feeling like a victim into feeling victorious because you have fought your way back to a meaningful life.

As humans, we do have ultimate control of our forest, which is the way we choose to see the world. We can transform from prey to hunter. We can also choose to plant the seeds we have been given in that forest. The seeds we plant and the effort we give to nurturing the seedling sometimes develop as we reflect on our own suffering, but we can recognize that our struggles help us build deep reservoirs of strength to move past that suffering. We have control of our destiny. We can choose to develop many mighty trees, taking control by directing the development of the forests of our lives.

Summary

Through our own ambition, whatever it may be, we can build on a foundation of the adaptive spiral. It will take personal confidence and motivation, effort and action, as we explore the possibilities with our newly altered bodies. But if we can be persistent, we will go on to develop competencies, achievement, growth, and healthy relationships with others. Although no one has a crystal ball to predict your outcome, each of us has significant potential to unlock. In later chapters, I will outline some keys to help you on your way.

CHAPTER 7

WHAT IS "STROKE"? DEMYSTIFYING THE MYTHS

There are some things which cannot be learned quickly, and time, which is all we have, must be paid heavily for their acquiring.

— Ernest Hemingway

Of all the major health problems, stroke may be the least understood in the general population, an alarming statement in spite of stroke being the fifth most frequent cause of death in the United States, and the second leading cause of death worldwide. Perhaps a more important figure is how many people survive a stroke, most with permanent neurologic effects. More than 5 million people are living with the neurological scars from stroke in the United States. Stroke, in fact, usually does not kill the victim—stroke maims the person. The severity of the injuries is dependent on a number of factors. Some factors are physical and some psychological; some you will have control over—others you will not. It is critically important to understand what stroke is, and what it's not. This firm, deep appreciation and understanding may be the first step in navigating a successful recovery, which starts with what you *think* of stroke. A healthy paradigm about stroke will provide you with a roadmap of the way forward.

Although most people have a general idea of what stroke is, in many people's minds, stroke is shrouded in mystery. Some even have superstitious beliefs about it. Public service campaigns have helped in educating the public, yet stroke remains a surprisingly difficult concept for people to comprehend. The reason for this confusion is understandable.

The brain houses many functions we consider unique to humans. It controls personality, memory, reason, and judgment, resulting from complex brain processes, modified by a sophisticated and elaborate cascade of neurotransmitters in the brain. Truly, the human brain is the most scientifically elegant thing we have discovered in the entire universe.

Throughout time, the event we now designate as stroke has been called by many different names and has also been falsely attributed to a variety of things throughout the ages. Perhaps humankind has tried to explain the natural world in the most advanced thinking of the day, only to fall short. Historically, the word *apoplexy* was used to describe stroke. Of Greek origin, apoplexy is common to many languages and means to *strike with violence*. Later, because it seemed to some observers that the stroke patient looked as though he had been "struck by lightning," the medical term for stroke inferred a strike of lighting or a strike from the heavens.

The belief that God was connected to both good and bad events in human lives pervaded ancient people's thoughts, from weather patterns to health and disease, leading to many misinterpretations of cause and effect. Because human autopsy was forbidden, little understanding existed of what actually caused a stroke and its mysterious symptoms, leading people to be prone to superstition.

Not until the 1600s, when Swiss physician Johann Jakob Wepfer was granted permission to perform several autopsies, did the cause of stroke begin to be uncovered. In 1658, Wepfer published his observations of humans who had died from stroke. He stated, "I set forth that apoplexy is produced because the afflux [flow] of blood through the arteries is denied to the brain."[1] Therefore, anything that interrupted blood flowing to the brain, he correctly theorized, would produce apoplexy or stroke. What was mysterious for so many centuries basically came down to a plumbing problem—clogs and leaks—but with devastating consequences. It was discovered that internal bleeding in the brain could produce this kind of interruption of blood flow. Later, it was also theorized that a blocked artery could produce this interruption of blood flow, forming the rationale for the two categories of stroke. (However, the mechanisms of *why* these arteries become blocked in the first place was not discovered for another couple of hundred years.)

About the same time, again in the study of human anatomy, Thomas Willis discovered that the arteries inside the brain, oddly, form a *circle*. Thomas aptly named his discovery the "Circle of Willis," which provides a partial redundancy to blocked blood passageways. He correctly theorized that if it were not for this circle with its redundant blood flow, the effect of stroke would be more catastrophic or even universally fatal. Later, it was recognized that stroke on one side of the brain produced paralysis on the opposite side of the body. In the 1800s, it was discovered that these arteries around the brain could be clogged by thickening of the arteries, called arteriosclerosis, or by a clot traveling through the bloodstream and ending in the brain. Clots of this type are called emboli.[2]

Simple Plumbing of the Brain

Today, we know stroke is divided into two general categories. When an artery becomes occluded from a clot formed *inside* the brain, the clot is called a thrombus. Alternatively, when a clot travels through the blood and enters the brain, causing an occlusion, the clot is called an embolus. Clot-based strokes, whether the clot forms in the brain or elsewhere in the body, are grouped together and called *ischemic stroke*. Ischemic stroke represents about 85 percent of all stroke cases. The second category occurs when an artery bursts within the brain. Arteries burst due to a number of factors, such as hypertension, or they can just burst spontaneously, causing bleeding or hemorrhage. As a category, strokes due to arteries that burst are called *hemorrhagic stroke*; this type of stroke accounts for 15 percent of cases.

Much has been written about methods to reverse the effects of stroke in the first hours of symptom onset. And, indeed, more advanced techniques are being discovered and confirmed all the time. For example, an intravenous medication called tPA, or tissue plasminogen activator, has been around since the late 1990s and is a strong blood thinner that can sometimes break up a clot that has formed within a person's bloodstream and lodged itself within the brain.

A popular educational slogan regarding stroke in the United States is "Time is Brain." This means specifically that the more time that passes from stroke symptom onset, the more irreversible damage to the brain is done. For the last couple of decades, the best medical knowledge was that a three-hour window exists to administer tPA before the risks outweigh the benefits. In fact, it has been well-established over many studies that one of the most important factors in stroke recovery is whether or not the patient received tPA, which is based on how much time had passed since symptom onset.

It's important to remember that tPA is only appropriate in clot-based (or ischemic strokes), which represent roughly 85 percent of all strokes. The main risk of tPA is, in fact, *bleeding*, so it's important to get a quick CT scan of the head before giving tPA. Later, it was discovered to be more effective to deliver the tPA from a catheter pushed up through the artery to the brain, thereby bathing the clot with tPA. A few devices can retrieve the clot (called thrombectomy) that caused the stroke and restore blood flow, again through a catheter pushed up to the brain's arteries. The three-hour window has been extended for these special procedures to sixteen hours and even twenty-four hours in certain situations, allowing doctors to offer stroke patients more options in the first hours of stroke. These procedures seldom totally reverse the stroke's effects, but they do drastically reduce the number and severity of the symptoms that remain in the short- and long-term.

Dr. Jennifer Majersik, Director of the Neurology Stroke Center at the University of Utah, says:

> [T]here are so many things we can do in the first several hours of stroke onset. The problem for many stroke patients is access to a hospital where they can do these advanced procedures quickly. Knowing what hospitals are stroke centers in your area is very important. Many smaller hospitals with limited resources can still provide top-notch stroke care by using consulting services such as telestroke, which provides immediate stroke expertise to under-served areas. The health and function of your brain may depend on these services.[3]

In my outpatient clinic, I see one particular man I will call Brett, who is now in his mid-forties and who had the same type of stroke as mine. Many factors go into the equation of stroke recovery, but for Brett, one of those factors is that he was unable to get tPA because by the time he and his family knew that his symptoms represented a stroke, it was too late for tPA to be effective. Just as there are a multitude of unique brains, a multitude of factors influence brain recovery. Brett was in a rural town and was slow to get to the hospital, so by the time he got to the ER, it was past the three-hour window, which meant Brett had to face a steep, uphill recovery battle.

After five years, Brett still has severe speech disabilities and can only make a single one-syllable sound. Amazingly, his comprehension is superb. He is able to walk sufficiently well, but with significant muscle tightness on the right side of his body. Despite all of this, he has enrolled in the vocational rehabilitation program offered by the state and is now completing coursework for an architecture drafting program. Brett is making the most of his life, even amid medical trials with his deficits from the stroke.

Brett teaches us a couple of important things. First, he has a good understanding of what stroke is. He does not get hung up on questions like, "*Why* did this happen?" and "*Why* me?" Truthfully, up to one-third of stroke patients never do learn exactly *why* the stroke occurred. It becomes important to move past *why* questions to continue on in your life's purpose.

The second important thing Brett teaches us is not to look back and wonder, "What if I had received more expert care in the early stages of the stroke? What if I had been able to receive tPA?" There may be guilt or shame—directed at yourself or someone close to you. If this is the case, stop it now. Doing so may be the only way to move on to healing and recovery. Among the various degrees of stroke severity are a multitude of paths to recovery. Some of those factors are physical, some cognitive, and some psychological. But one thing is true in most cases of stroke: You may have more control than you think. These paths to recovery all start when you can begin to look forward, not backward. These paths to recovery all start with a *decision* to make your personal best effort to recover function for the purpose of achieving the highest quality of life available to you.

It is, admittedly, a daunting task to attempt to help the brain heal itself after the devastation of a stroke. Even if the stroke's effects are quite mild, they are deeply personal, and usually accompanied by changes in function, speech, and cognition, along with effects on family and social roles, career, and overall independence. Nevertheless, most of the time there is reason for hope. There is reason for effort, for climbing that hill and, in some cases, of scaling that mountain.

Today, though there is still much to discover about the brain's function and repair, the science of the last century has yielded incredible knowledge about this remarkable organ. Notably, the centers of control for all of the body's functions have been identified. The interplay within different regions of the brain is now understood. Additionally, factors that can help brain recovery have been identified.

The brain, in most cases, has a remarkable ability to repair a portion of the damage and, partially or completely, compensate for the devastating deficits of stroke and other forms of acquired brain injury. Physicians like myself in the field of physical medicine and rehabilitation, along with a whole cadre of neuro-rehabilitation therapists, nurses, psychologists, and social workers, are here to guide patients through the sometimes complex path of recovery. The neuro-rehab team is specifically trained and oriented to facilitate the maximum amount of recovery possible, given the unique circumstances that every stroke patient faces. In other words, our focus is on helping individuals achieve their maximum potential. In this sense, rehabilitation professionals have a critical and humbling role of getting people back on their feet. We strive for neurological recovery for the purpose of facilitating and fostering greater quality of life.

It's important to have clarity on the process of stroke. There should be no shame, nor wondering and dwelling on *"Why me?"* We can move on to recovery and greater quality of life.

Hard, painful work lies before us. In a sense, stroke is pain, pure and simple. There is no easy way around the fact. The late author Carlfred Broderick, who eventually lost his fight with cancer, said, "I'm certain that pain destroys and embitters far more often than it ennobles. I'm certain injustice is destructive of good things far more than people are able to rise above it. I'm not saying that pain is good. Pain is terrible."[4] However, Broderick goes on to say pain and suffering teach us lessons we can learn no other way. When possible, it's important to leave whatever pain we can *behind us*, and to realize that we choose whether to fight or succumb (flight) in this unjust world. The mind's ability to choose our response—fight or succumb—is the principal reason it is so important to understand stroke. Stroke boils down to a very complex *plumbing* problem. That's it. No more. Nothing supernatural. It's important to understand this fact so we can put all our energy into the fight that lies before us.

Stroke does not produce the excruciatingly physical type of pain. It does bring pain and suffering to individuals who experience stroke and those who love them. I wonder if a tree feels any pain when being pruned, or when a violent windstorm breaks off a major branch. A great deal of our growth, much like a tree, happens when we choose to endure and struggle through pain, whether it's physical or emotional. If we choose to step beyond what feels comfortable and do the work that seems hard, that pain will not break us, but make us wiser. We can recognize the beauty even in things that are broken and in places that are not whole.

It is important to dispel misbeliefs and understand the true cause of stroke—that it is a natural, though devastating, part of many people's lives. Stroke is not something supernatural, even though those thoughts may creep into our minds on occasion. In the end, it becomes important to find beauty in oneself, even beauty in imperfect things and the places that are broken.

Summary

When trying to understand a complex and life-altering stroke, it is tempting to assign false causation or ruminate on "what if" scenarios. However, those false beliefs are a barrier to your ability to progress. When we are able to dispel these thoughts from our minds, we can move forward with confidence.

CHAPTER 8

PREVENTION AND NEW FRONTIERS

We are responsible for our own health, but we are not the ones to blame for our illnesses.

— Elisabeth Kübler-Ross

We all are going to age. Unwelcome things will happen to our bodies. The questions for each of us are: What can we do now to try to prevent the sometimes severe consequences of living with a body that breaks down over time? For those of us who have had stroke in the past, how do we minimize our risk, while at the same time, emotionally and psychologically move on?

Stroke is perceived primarily as a disease of the elderly. However, even among people 15–44 years of age, stroke is still reported to be a significant cause of death. More than one-third of those who experience stroke are under age sixty-five, and about 10 percent of stroke cases happen to people under the age of fifty, causing brutal long-term effects—stroke is the leading cause of major disability.

How do you take responsibility for your own health in the future, but let go of the blame that one naturally feels creeping in after experiencing debilitating illnesses?

Frontiers in Life

We all have experiences that push us out of our comfort zones. If you are living with the effects of stroke, you may feel like every day is a battle, every hour a new struggle. You left the comfort of your old life behind and headed off to a new frontier, a frontier where you struggle, where you encounter fear, where you face hardship. Perhaps it's often on those frontiers in life that we are most alive. On those frontiers we learn wisdom, find joy, and discover meaning and purpose in our work. Stroke can be one of those frontiers. The challenge is simultaneously doing the hard work of recovery while making changes in lifestyle to prevent another health event.

To the five million stroke survivors in this country, know that you are not alone. Your stroke was not by choice, but it is the frontier you find yourself on.

The first thing on many of your minds is: How do I prevent this from happening again? This question is completely appropriate, and it does *not* equate to looking backwards, but to being proactive with your health for the future. This active approach for stroke risk-factor reduction can also lead to other areas of health maintenance and wellbeing. In fact, even if you have had a stroke, your risk of another stroke is far less that your risk for a heart-related health problem. Fortunately, stroke and heart disease have many common risk factors, so taking steps to reduce your risk factors for one will naturally reduce risk of the other. Knowing what to do to reduce the risk of stroke and heart disease is one important aspect of moving on with your life. You will be faced with a whole cadre of new things to think about—avoiding complications, modifying your lifestyle to more healthy choices, and putting the anxieties of the past in their place. Only then will you be able to move on to new frontiers.

Whether you're young or old, male or female, a billionaire, a statesman, unemployed, or an athlete, two things will be critical to your stroke recovery: 1) avoiding unnecessary complications, and 2) embracing new possibilities, thereby maximizing your individual potential.

Control What Can Be Controlled

Stroke and heart disease are not the only complications to have on your mind. There are other complications in the months after stroke to be aware of, both to know what to watch out for and to seek prompt treatment if one of these complications comes up. These complications are addressed in Chapter 14.

The prevention of stroke in someone who has already had a stroke is called *secondary prevention*. Secondary prevention is regarded as an integral part of stroke rehabilitation, as important as walking, functional skills, or swallowing disorders. Alternatively, successful, long-term secondary prevention helps to maintain regained function by reducing future strokes.

Secondary prevention entails all the things you can do to decrease the chances of another stroke or a health-related health problem. It's helpful to put risk factors into two buckets: those we cannot do anything about, and those we can. Things we can't change include our age, gender, race, and heredity. For example, risk of stroke approximately doubles every decade past age fifty. So, a sixty-year-old would have double the risk of stroke as a fifty-year-old. But we cannot turn back the clock; some risks we just incur by nature of growing older.

We can, however, do something about a wide number of stroke risk factors. For example, about 25 percent of the US adult population has high blood pressure (hypertension). Over time, hypertension increases the risk of stroke about fourfold. Public campaigns have attempted to address the major risk factors of hypertension—with good success. Over the last forty years since these campaigns have been underway, stroke rates have made moderate improvements. The risk factors that *can be changed* are called modifiable risk factors, and they deserve some attention. Incidentally, paying attention and adapting your lifestyle to correspond to these modifiable risk factors would make you feel better and healthier.

Again, it's important not to look back on the past and blame yourself for things like *not* perfectly addressing your hypertension. In my clinical practice, I see a lot of people who beat themselves up over not paying attention to the risk factors before the stroke happened. Honestly, give yourself a break. In your pre-stroke life, you had many pressing and urgent demands and were doing the best you could. Now it is important to start with a clean slate, today, to make the changes necessary to support optimal health.

For example, pay attention when your doctor says you have a heart condition called atrial fibrillation, or AFib. AFib is a condition where two of the four chambers of the heart beat very rapidly. When the chambers beat this rapidly and without the heart's usual coordination, it can create the environment within your heart for blood clots to form, break from, and travel up to the brain, causing a stroke. AFib is more likely as you age, and it can create a profound risk of stroke; the presence of AFib incurs an 8% risk of stroke per year. At my rehabilitation center, we routinely screen for AFib in patients with a stroke because it can increase your risk of a second stroke fourfold. The usual and important treatment for AFib is blood thinners—something to talk to your doctor about if the suspicion arises.

Of course, it's a well-known fact that smoking raises your risk of stroke and a whole number of other things. If you smoke, stop now; don't beat yourself up, and move on.

With some of the risk factors for stroke, you may have carefully weighed the risks and benefits that eventually led to your stroke. For example, estrogen-based birth control pills (oral contraceptives) have a slight risk of stroke. Alternately, the state of pregnancy and childbirth also incurs a slight risk of stroke. These are not usually things we think about, nor should we base our life decisions on the possibility and fear of stroke. We have to live our lives. However, when moving on from an ischemic stroke, it's important to use a different form of contraception to lessen the future risk of stroke.

Additionally, if you have a clotting disorder (sometimes called a *hypercoagulable state*), it is important to consult with your doctor to determine the best form of blood thinner, if your doctor recommends one of these medications.

Alcohol can lead to hypertension, hypercoagulability, reduced cerebral blood flow, and increased risk for atrial fibrillation, thereby increasing risk of stroke. However, when restricted to light amounts, alcohol, especially red wine, can have a protective effect against stroke (one drink per day for women and two drinks per day for men).

Drugs of abuse, including cocaine, amphetamines, and heroin, are associated with a 6.5-fold increased risk for stroke.[1] If you have had a stroke associated with these types of addictive behaviors, it is especially important to seek the guidance of an appropriate counseling agency. Your doctor should be able to refer you to someone who can help.

Diet and exercise lead the list of what may be termed "healthy lifestyle factors." These factors include doing things that will not lead to obesity and inactivity, such as overeating and eating foods with processed sugar, which may lead to diabetes—another risk factor for stroke.

Obesity is more common after stroke than one might think. Obesity is linked to the very risk factors we want to avoid, such as hypertension diabetes mellitus, and high cholesterol.

Abdominal obesity has specifically been shown to be a risk factor for stroke among all racial groups. The American Heart Association recommends weight reduction be considered for all overweight stroke patients, to maintain a goal of a body mass index (BMI) of between 18.5 and 24.9 kg/m2. Addressing weight loss in stroke patients can be done through a combination of diet modification and exercise.

Proper nutrition is also a critical aspect of secondary prevention of stroke and health maintenance. An unhealthy diet can result in a poor cholesterol profile. Furthermore, unhealthy diet impairs the body's ability to detoxify itself or repair damaged cells, which is sometimes called oxidative stress.

A diet, such as the Cretan Mediterranean diet, that is high in beneficial oils (from olive, canola, and fish), legumes, fruits, and vegetables of all *colors* high in vitamins and antioxidants and low in cholesterol, transfat, and harmful animal fat lowers the risk of cardiovascular events. This Cretan diet also contains much less meat, but contains moderate amounts of fish and moderate amounts of red wine. The Cretan diet has been shown to reduce risk of stroke and heart attack by up to 60 percent in four years compared with the normal diet the American Heart Association recommends.[2]

However, a change in diet requires a change in *behavior* for an entire family. In my experience, changing diet habits is one of the hardest changes to make after stroke. Perhaps, making diet changes, or *any* changes for that matter, becomes more difficult as we age and get set in our ways. Certainly, changing your diet is more difficult than taking a few new medications, which takes only a few seconds each day; a new diet requires a categorical shift in shopping habits, meal preparation, and diet choices. Thus, out of all the recommendations after stroke, in my clinical experience, diet changes seem to be the "hardest nut to crack." Most Americans may always prefer an American diet and to eat what they want. Therefore, at our stroke rehabilitation center, we educate patients and family members on diet choices and follow up with additional guidance on the outpatient setting in our health and wellness programs. We find that this level of support is both helpful and necessary to create positive changes in behavior, for people who *want* to change.

Exercise makes up the second prong of a healthy lifestyle. After stroke, barriers to exercise and healthy activity exist for individuals who have had a stroke. Public embarrassment and shame, as well as physical, transportation, speech, and cognitive difficulties, often prevent stroke survivors from being as active as they should and want to be. Without assistance to overcome these barriers, stroke patients often become inactive after their formal outpatient therapy is over.

This pattern of inactivity often leads to secondary complications, such as poor cardiac fitness, muscle atrophy, and osteoporosis. Recent studies have shown, however, that aggressive therapy, even years after stroke, increases aerobic fitness, muscle strength, and overall function.

Substantial evidence exists on the beneficial effects physical activity has on multiple risk factors for stroke, including improved blood pressure and weight, and lowering the risk of diabetes. The goals of the physical conditioning program include regaining pre-stroke levels of activity, preventing recurrent stroke or cardiovascular events, and improving fitness.[3] Stroke patients capable of engaging in physical activity should be encouraged to perform at least thirty minutes of moderate intensity physical exercise 3-7 days a week.

Avoid Maladaptive Spirals

Unfortunately, physiological and emotional barriers frequently exist after stroke. These barriers limit physical activity and maintenance of healthy lifestyles. Stroke patients should be actively counseled and provided with resources to encourage healthy lifestyles.

Of all the risk factors—those you can control and those you cannot—perhaps the biggest is one you have complete control over. But rather than being a medical risk factor, it is mostly psychological. I worry about this risk factor with many of my patients who are just being released from the inpatient rehabilitation unit after stroke. The worry is that the patient will have an affinity for his or her couch—that fear and discouragement will be too paralyzing for them to find a reason to try, a reason for hope. The *couch factor* of inactivity and overeating represents a major *maladaptive spiral* of inactivity, poor mood, unhealthy eating, and obesity. This maladaptive spiral leads to other health problems and, if it is not corrected, could result in death. But the power is within each of us to break the maladaptive cycle.

In *The Seven Habit of Highly Effective People*, Stephen Covey wrote about the need to create a healthy balanced life when he proposed that each of us needs to "sharpen the saw." *Sharpen the saw* means, among other things, take the time to exercise and eat a nutritious diet on a regular basis, which helps people in a number of ways. Covey said:

> Probably the greatest benefit you will experience from exercising will be the development of your habit of…proactivity [your feeling of being the hunter, not the prey]. As you act based on the value of physical well-being instead of reacting to all the forces that keep you from exercising [physical and psychological barriers], your paradigm of yourself, your self-esteem, your self-confidence, and your integrity will be profoundly affected.[4]

Over time, these *sharpen the saw* skills can become a powerful attribute, and part of your character. These skills will serve you in many ways, and may, in fact, keep you alive.

Early in my career, I treated a bright, twenty-six-year-old woman who had suffered a major brainstem stroke that had left half her body paralyzed. It was a devastating blow to her. She did the typical inpatient rehabilitation, and we tried to prepare her as best we could for what lay ahead. She left the hospital after several weeks, but she still was unable to walk, had a feeding tube, and would go on to develop severe tight muscle spasms (spasticity) over one-half of her body. At home, understandably, she struggled with depression and anxiety. She was unwilling to try anything. Her sense of hope seemed lost. We were all worried about her. Then, through a special relationship she had developed with one of our therapists, she developed the courage to go on one of our outdoor adaptive recreation rafting trips. That started a slow but steady unwinding of the maladaptive spiral she was in, and she began to do the things important to an adaptive spiral. More confidence led to more competence and capability. She started walking for exercise with a group of stroke survivors. She started to go to counseling, she responded well to an anti-anxiety medication, she came to medical appointments to get her spasticity under control, and slowly, she became more comfortable in the community and with social interactions. She eventually started a modified biking program with the same group of stroke survivors and was able to achieve many great things.

Ten years later, she has now found a high quality of life; she is married and has had her first child. It took a long time for her to get out of that dark place, spending too much time on her couch, and unwind from the downward spiral she was in, but every tiny and large step forward represents a major success. We are all happy and proud of her successes, and as she keeps sharpening her saw, her success will just breed more successes.

This is my wish for every person who has been affected by a stroke.

Summary

You did not choose the new frontier you and your family find yourselves in. However, you are not alone; many people have passed this way before. It is important to change what you can to lower your risk factors. That change involves adopting a healthy lifestyle that includes smoking cessation, maintaining a healthy body weight, and maintaining a physically active life. It is important to manage key risk factors such as hypertension, diabetes mellitus, high cholesterol, and atrial fibrillation, which have been associated with an increased risk of developing another stroke. We can only do our best, nothing more, but there is hope for a rich, full life.

CHAPTER 9

LANGUAGE CENTER: THE ROCKET SCIENTIST AND THE ELOQUENT TISSUE OF THE BRAIN

Speech has power. Words do not fade. What starts out as a sound, ends in a deed.

— Abraham Joshua Herschel

Although all of our brain structures are important, we sometimes talk of the very most critical portions of the brain as the "eloquent tissue." These eloquent tissues are most often those structures that contain the key to language and speech. In part, this suggests what we hold most dear as humans—the ability to communicate with others using language.

For purposes of simplicity, I will be referring to the left side of the brain as the dominant side, housing the language center. Interestingly, in actuality, 10 percent of people are left-handed, but even among left-handers, 50 percent still have their left brain as the dominant hemisphere. Thus, except for rare cases, the language centers are on the left side of the brain (but these rare variants do exist).

Language as a Communication Tool

Before we discuss language, we must decide what language is. Language has been called the foundation of civilization. Written and spoken language are the sharp tools we use at times of love and peace, as well as in anger and war. Language is made up of symbols called letters and words that the brain interprets into patterns that express meaning and emotion. Indeed, when I hear "I love you," it reminds me that I have a soul. Loss of language is truly devastating.

When lying alone in a quiet space, one may think in a continuous stream of internal speech. At such times, language seems to be an integral part of *thought*. But no evidence exists that language is essential to any particular intellectual process.

Damage to the brain for many stroke patients results in a complete loss of language, both external (speaking) and internal (thinking in terms of words). However, researchers have been unable to correlate this loss with loss of intelligence or cognition. In his book *Origins of the Modern Mind*, Merlin Donald compares the loss of language in stroke patients to the loss of a *sensory system*. The patients have lost a system or tool that greatly simplifies life in the world, but like a blind or deaf person, there is no diminished intellect or consciousness that accompanies this loss.

Language is thought to be a method of communicating the information *within* thoughts. One experiment used to demonstrate this idea involves research participants who listen to a short passage of several sentences. The participants are then asked to repeat the passage. Most participants accurately convey the gist of the passage in the sentences they produce, but they do not come close to repeating the sentences verbatim. It appears as if two transformations have occurred: 1) Upon hearing the passage, the participants convert the language of the passage into a more *abstract representation* of its meaning; 2) in order to recreate the passage, the participants recall this representation and convert its meaning back into language.[1]

This separation of thought and language is a difficult concept to wrap your head around, a concept most of us are never forced to think about. Yet when the language center is damaged by a stroke, these concepts become hyper-relevant. Indeed, most people take it for granted that language is a powerful tool with which to manipulate their thoughts; it provides a method to privately rehearse, analyze, and modify thoughts. Language allows us to apply a common set of codes and symbols—words—to our own ideas and the ideas of others, through the means of speech, writing, gestures, and even facial expressions. However, many stroke patients have experienced this separation, one where thoughts do exist even though the patient may be mute. For these patients, the dual concepts of working toward maximum neurologic recovery and finding successful adaptation strategies is of utmost importance.

Broca's Area of the Brain

Phillip Lieberman, a cognitive scientist at Brown University, has investigated the origin of speech for many years and has used this research to form hypotheses about the evolution of language. Even before the development of speech, there must have first been a *desire* to communicate. Purposeful communication requires a coordinated transmitter and an attentive receiver. The first form of such communication may have been through hand gestures and facial expressions. Reading facial expressions may have helped individuals anticipate the coming actions of their peers. Attention to hand movements and gestures may have allowed copying of skills requiring manual dexterity such as tool making.

Lieberman also suggests that speech improved greatly about 150,000 years ago with some evolutionary changes in the throat that made key vowel sounds possible. Thus, language has evolved over many centuries to the form of our modern language, but it still requires two willing communicators. Purposeful, deliberate willingness to communicate is sometimes lost when a stroke makes speaking arduous, frustrating, and difficult. Often, the stroke patient has to fight and struggle to recover this vital skill, sometimes over years or even decades.

A key to understand is how the brain interacts with language to make communication possible. Paul Broca, a scientist-physician born in France in 1824, was the first to discover the quintessential center in the brain for expressive communication; when this area is damaged, it causes expressive aphasia or Broca's aphasia, which is a form of "non-fluent aphasia." Thus, this undesirable condition will forever be linked to his name.

Damage to the left lower portion of the frontal lobe, or Broca's area, will impair a patient's ability to express language, though their ability to understand language is preserved. It's as if the capacity to express thoughts and desires is locked in a lockbox, though what people say is perfectly understandable. This creates a most frustrating situation for many stroke patients.

Broca discovered this situation by studying the brains of people with speech and language disorders resulting from brain injuries, such as stroke. Eventually, Broca heard of a patient who had a loss of speech and paralysis but not a loss of comprehension nor mental function. The patient was unable to produce any words other than "tan." When the patient died, Broca performed an autopsy. He determined that, as he predicted, the patient did have damage to the left lower frontal lobe. For the next two years, Broca went on to find autopsy evidence from twelve more cases in support of the localization of articulated language. Interestingly, Paul Broca died at age fifty-six of a burst artery, causing a hemorrhagic stroke. Even a pioneer of discovery was not immune from the life-threatening effects of stroke.

Language acquisition is one of the most fundamental and important human traits. During our years of language acquisition as infants, the brain not only stores language information but also adapts to language's dialects. This underappreciated fact shows that the brain can indeed change itself through deliberate, intentional activity. We also know that the adult brain has the ability to adapt, which bears special significance on the potential for language skill recovery after stroke.

Isolation When the Communication Tool Is Lost

When I was a young resident, one of the first stroke patients I cared for was an astrophysicist named Keith, literally a rocket scientist, who designed rocket systems for NASA. While at home one day, fifty-four-year-old Keith collapsed and developed a semi-conscious state. The paramedics rushed him to the University Hospital where it was discovered that he had a major hemorrhage in the left side of his brain, a life-threatening condition. He received advanced medical care and regained full consciousness over the next couple of days, only to find that his right arm and leg were completely paralyzed. What's more, he was mute…but could understand simple and even complex things that were said to him. The hemorrhagic stroke he had experienced damaged the Broca's area of the brain within the language center. Keith became a rocket scientist who literally lost contact with his ground control.

Having worked for years in the space exploration field and being a bright scientist himself, Keith was disconnected from the world by his expressive aphasia, which typically affects all forms of expression—verbal, written, and even gestures. As a young resident who had suffered a similar type of stroke, I wondered if he felt like he had a circuit that was "dead" in his spacecraft; thereby, communication had been lost within his world. Did he feel like I felt, in seclusion, even though there were people all around him, having lost the ability to access the words to express meaning to your loved ones? Was his hospital bed his floating spacecraft, far above the earth? Or did he feel "at-one" with the universe, as Jill Bolte, PhD, a brain scientist, described in her memoir *Stroke of Insight*. Bolte points out that many people describe having a stroke as a surreal experience, especially when the stroke involves the brain's left hemisphere. The left hemisphere broadly relates to language, logic, and reasoning. To have a stroke in this region of the brain can produce a feeling that the individual is in another dimension. They may be unable to speak, even as they feel themselves drifting farther and farther away from planet earth, in the quiet of their spacecraft, in the most severe isolation, floating, floating away….

I have been there, in that very quiet and somewhat dark place. I certainly didn't realize how much I relied on that tool of language to connect me to the outside world. At the time of my stroke, never had I felt such weakness and isolation. Complete and utter isolation. My spaceship was quietly drifting away from planet earth. I fully comprehended it.

Similar to my experience, the professionals on Keith's stroke rehabilitation team, like myself, began slowly to reel Keith back to earth. But Keith did the hard work of recovery—as hard as he was able.

And today he speaks fine, though a little slowly, and communicates well, which is further evidence of the brain's ability to adapt through deliberate, intentional activity. Keith says today, "I felt empowered at times to do things beyond my normal strength." He eventually found meaning and a new reprieve and freedom from isolation and frustration through nature photography. Photographing the western states' National Parks gave him a renewed sense of quality of life.

At other times, some patients retain profound speech impairments. For those individuals, use of assistive-technology for speech through a computer system is often an effective and useful strategy that provides a vital aid to communication and tethers them back to planet earth.

By any means, it is important to seek education for patients and especially families about language disorders after stroke, recovery potential, and optimal ways to communicate with patients with aphasia.

The Primitive Brain's Contribution to Language

I treat a wonderful man from a delightful family I have known since my youth. He is in his eighties now, and several years ago, he had a severe stroke in the left middle cerebral artery, completely knocking out the Broca's language center and paralyzing his right side. He struggled with his speech and language, as *all* forms of expressive language were affected—even writing, gestures, and facial expression. Weeks became months, which became years, but still no speech production. He was mute—with one exception: He could utter just a few curse words. Swearing was not part of this good family man's character before the stroke. His swearing caught his conservative, God-fearing family off-guard. But, day after day, he could only express himself using these two or three words, said in different tones to add emphasis when needed—words that all who were close to him would find offensive. Why does this strange phenomenon occur, one that has puzzled family members and scientists for centuries?

The answer probably lies in the brain's deep and primitive regions, specifically in the limbic system. Perhaps we can gain insight into this by looking at a non-stroke condition called Tourette's syndrome. Tourette's syndrome is a troubling and generally poorly understood condition where the patient has subconscious impulses to engage in certain unwanted behaviors, such as "tics," shouting vulgarities, or howling. These behaviors come from the limbic system, which expresses emotions, drives, instincts, and impulses. In the limbic system is a primitive type of speech center, which activates when, for example, a dog barks, or, in the case of a Tourette's syndrome patient, when a person has howling behaviors. In the stroke patient with severe expressive aphasia, the limbic system primitive speech center also accounts for the vulgar cursing of otherwise mute men and women. An understanding of this fairly common phenomenon will hopefully give some peace to confused family members confronted with this problem.

An Aphasic Writer

In cases where verbal speech does not come back adequately, sometimes other forms of communication do return, such as writing. Ann is among the kindest, most generous, and most patient women I know. She has severe expressive aphasia. Now in her mid-sixties, if she takes her time, she can slowly form some words. However, her mind is active, exploring new worlds in creative, virtuous concepts that she writes as children's literature. I am amazed by her deep and powerful thoughts, expressed in stories for children, and in her ability to compensate for the interactions she would like to have with the outside world. Her language circuit is certainly *not* "dead."

Summary

The desire to communicate is strong in humans, and language provides a powerful tool by which to communicate. Although language is not required for complex cognitive thoughts, it is without a doubt helpful in aiding an individual's internal thoughts, allowing for a host of powerful mental operations. When language abilities are lost with expressive aphasia, a profound sense of isolation often develops. Language abilities usually vastly improve after stroke, but it's up to patients, family members, and their support networks to fight off emotional despondency and misinformation, and help the patient to adapt successfully.

CHAPTER 10

WERNICKE'S APHASIA AND THE COWBOY POET

There is something about words.... Inside you they work their magic.

— Diane Setterfield, *The Thirteenth Tale*

Language as Art

The enormous variety of art created in human societies throughout the world expresses a multitude of ideas, experiences, cultural concepts, creativity, and social values. The arts—particularly poetry, literature, opera, musicals, theater, and film—form a *communication system* between artist and viewer that often involves a representation of language. Whereas nearly everyone can use language, it's less common that an individual can create art using language with qualities that elicit reactions of pleasure and appreciation in other people. We call these individuals artists.

Perhaps the analogy of a message in a bottle is quite fitting; art may have more to do with the tides of the oceans than actual composition itself, but humans, nonetheless, are compelled to send their messages in a bottle out through language, and these messages often take on the form of art. Sometimes this ability is developed from years of labor in honing that skill, but occasionally, it happens spontaneously. Understanding art's underpinnings from a neurological standpoint is challenging, in part because it happens spontaneously. Perhaps clues and insights can be obtained from stroke patients who suddenly have their language skills stripped away. I am giving much attention to language in all its forms because language has so much to do with being human, of being a member of society. Moreover, the language deficits that arise after stroke are generally poorly understood by the general public and the medical community alike.

I explained Broca's aphasia in the previous chapter, but another type of aphasia exists with much different features—specifically features in language and in cognition, rather than in expression. Imagine a blood clot traveling through the arteries, up the neck, to the large blood vessels entering the brain. Winding in a convoluted path, similar to life, the clot makes its way up to the brain.

The largest vessel is the middle cerebral artery. Its left or right side produces vastly different effects in the body. Imagine the clot travels through the blood to the left main artery to branch off the trunk. The middle cerebral artery branches from a main trunk to two distinct branches, an upper and a lower branch. Although both of these branches affect language, the language deficits could not be more different. Upper or lower branch—by pure chance—would produce distinctly different speech and language problems. Luck of the draw…chance… will affect lives in completely different ways. If the lower branch is affected, the form of aphasia will be markedly different than that of the upper branch (which leads to Broca's aphasia). A message in a bottle is flowing through the bloodstream, and where it ends up—a matter of chance will produce markedly different effects.

Wernicke's Area of the Brain

Like Paul Broca, Carl Wernicke was born in the mid-nineteenth century and became a scientist-physician whose research led to a groundbreaking discovery—the localization of another brain function in language. Wernicke's aphasia, also known as receptive aphasia, is a devastating type of aphasia in which individuals have difficulty understanding written and spoken language. Similar to Broca's area, Wernicke's area of the brain has been named for its discoverer. Wernicke's area is also a left middle cerebral artery territory structure, located about four centimeters away from Broca's area. It resides at the back of the left temporal lobe of the brain, in the portion of the brain just above the left ear.

Patients with Wernicke's aphasia demonstrate near effortless speech output, though they make many errors in their speech, make up new nonsense words, and are typically unaware of their errors in speech or that it may lack meaning. In this form of aphasia, the patient is able to speak, but the words don't make any sense. Thus, the term "receptive aphasia" is sometimes used. The patient cannot understand, nor be understood, and has no insight into there being a communication problem at all.

Patients with this condition produce a large amount of speech without much meaning, and have a lack of language comprehension. Writing also tends to lack content or meaning. Patients typically remain unaware of even their most profound language deficits. Like many acquired language disorders in stroke, Wernicke's aphasia can be experienced in many different ways and to many different degrees. Severity levels may range from being unable to understand even the simplest spoken or written information to missing minor details of a conversation. Usually, patients with Wernicke's aphasia have difficulty with comprehension, working memory, and thinking (cognition). In most cases, deficits in strength (i.e., hemiparesis) do not occur in individuals with Wernicke's aphasia.

This loss of receptive language ability is truly devastating because without the recognition and awareness of the problem, individuals with Wernicke's aphasia often lack the ability to change and recover function. Because Wernicke's aphasia is partially a comprehension and cognition problem, the information in this chapter is primarily for caregivers and less for the stroke patient himself.

The Cowboy Poet Whose Words Lost Their Meaning

The rough-and-tumble cowboy on the open range represents the last remnant of the old West. Choosing to let themselves go where language melts into art, many of these cowboys come to appreciate the beauty of the landscapes that surround them, the solitude that life on the range brings, and the peace within their hearts—then their writing about their life takes rhyme and becomes poetry.

All this, while still engaged in back-breaking labor in the field. There is actually a growing number of cowboys sharing their skills of language with, at times, beautiful and meaningful poetry.

Some people are skilled at using language creatively, when words turn into phrases and develop into rhymes, which sometimes take the form of poems. The process is similar to making fire—and not the kind of fire that rains down from the heavens in the form of lightning. Rather, the discovery of a spark, the nurturing it into a flame, and then harnessing it into a sustainable fire.

I have encountered these cowboy-artists occasionally in my medical practice, but none so meaningful, yet tragically disheartening, as Chuck, who had flamed the fire of self-discovery in his poetry before a devastating stroke snuffed out that flame for a time. A Wyoming rancher, Chuck was sixty when a severe stroke literally made him fall off his horse. Smoking was a vice he never could give up. As a pastime, working long days, alone, on the ranch, Chuck had a lot of time to think. Words became rhymes, which became simple poems. With time, these poems came to mean a lot to him; some of these simple rhymes were too good, he thought, to just be lost. So he put pen to paper and wrote his spontaneous expressions of art. He kept his poetry to himself for many years, then self-consciously shared some of his works.

But when a stroke came to his door, his ability to wordsmith lines into poetry vanished, evaporated—his fire was doused. Language itself died that day. Language, mediated by patterns of neurons firing, from thoughts translated to words—which are mere symbols—speech and written language. Perhaps we all have some elements in us of the cowboy poet.

Chuck began speaking using gibberish, "word-salad," or nonsense words. He also had poor comprehension of what was being said to him, as well as poor insight into the fact that he was talking gibberish, consistent with Wernicke's aphasia. Wernicke's aphasia is a form of "fluent aphasia," meaning the effort and melody of speech is easy to produce and fluent, but in no way is the speech itself truly fluent—Wernicke's patients usually have a severe deficit in comprehension, cognition, and insight into their speech problems.

When Chuck was released from the hospital, his family chose to stay in the Salt Lake area for a few months to capitalize on the intense specialized therapy; they wanted Chuck to regain as much neurological recovery as possible in our outpatient therapy clinic. I spent the majority of my time talking to and educating his wife and daughter on the progress they were seeing, checking on any agitation that might be present, and developing strategies that might be helpful.

When a loved one has Wernicke's aphasia, a few things are important to know from the start. They will usually go through different phases that, in my experience, are predictable. In the first phase, the patient is neither understanding what is said to them nor do they comprehend that what they are being told doesn't make sense to them, and they are speaking in gibberish themselves. In other words, they lack the comprehension of language and the *insight* that something is wrong with their comprehension. Eventually, they gain some element of insight into their problems with language, usually because people around them are not appropriately responding to their directions. This starts the second phase as frustration sets in. The third stage commences when frustration leads to anxiety, agitation, and other behavioral patterns. The fourth phase occurs when the patient has insight into the language problem and develops strategies to effectively cope with the situation.

Family members and loved ones can employ several strategies to ease the patient's frustration. Because patients will generally be able to understand facial expressions (of confusion or frustration vs. positive reassurances), I tell family members whenever possible to smile politely and with respect, and not to let their frustration feed the patient's frustration and agitation. Also, use soft, reassuring tones when addressing these patients, and don't fall into the common pattern of raising your voice to try to get the patient to understand. Lastly, avoid overwhelming the patient with visitors, noise, or unnecessary stimulation. With speech and cognitive therapy, their language and cognitive abilities will likely improve. These patients usually regain their ability to walk and use both arms. However, occasionally, these patients can present long-term challenges. Cognitively, they often need supervision for their safety; for example, they are prone to wander off and may get lost.

Luckily, Chuck didn't have any frustration that led to actual agitation, but I supplied the family with some medication just in case, which he never needed. Chuck's wife and daughter were almost perfect in the way they employed the strategies mentioned above. Adaptations were made to each of their lives. Chuck was eventually able to go back to his rural Wyoming home and live safely with his wife on their ranch, but his language skills—the ability to generate spontaneous speech that was often poetic—is unlikely to ever return. Hopefully, he will gain other meaningful and creative outlets to replace that poetry that has vanished in the wind.

Summary

Language powerfully moves people; when it is used as a form of art and then lost, for a time or permanently, it's especially devastating. Wernicke's aphasia is one type of aphasia that causes individuals to have difficulty understanding written and spoken language, to produce nonsense speech, and to have a poor understanding of their language problems. This loss of language function is due to damage in the left middle cerebral artery, and is usually not associated with severe hemiparesis. Through helpful strategies and the patience of caregivers and family members, these patients can have a safe and good quality of life in the home setting. Even in the case of Wernicke's aphasia, individuals and families can still foster a high, though different, quality of life.

CHAPTER 11

COGNITIVE SYNDROMES AFTER STROKE: RIGHT BRAIN SYNDROMES

Our greatest glory is not in never falling, but in getting up every time we fall.

— Confucius

For those who have suffered a stroke, or those who love someone who has had a stroke, deficits in thinking (cognition) or personality changes can be emotionally confusing and difficult to deal with. This chapter addresses the relatively common occurrence of cognitive and personality changes after stroke.

The Governing Center

Essentially, all humans have two brains: an evolutionarily primitive subconscious brain (sub-cortical brain structures) and a more recently developed advanced conscious brain (cerebral cortex). These two brains are normally tethered together and act fairly synergistically, keeping each other in check imperceptibly.

The cerebral cortex controls our conscious brain and houses all conscious thought, the goal-directed rational thoughts that lead to our behaviors—good or bad. The more primitive subconscious brain controls our subconscious thoughts. We typically have deliberate "veto" power over the primitive subconscious mind, both of our *behaviors* and of what we say, as we self-censor, thereby suppressing unconscious drives and behaviors. Most of us have this deliberate veto power because we have two functional frontal lobes. When stroke affects the left frontal lobe, the right frontal lobe has the capacity to take over for both frontal lobes. However, when the right hemisphere of the brain sustains damage, the evidence of the damage is readily apparent.

Let's examine how our attention and impulses are normally regulated. The brain, especially this governing center, processes many items of information out of view and under the surface. The brain is selective in what it allows to surface because we have a very finite amount of information we can consciously process at one time. Only a small fraction of the information reaches conscious thought. However, conscious thought is where we live our lives, how we remember to pay the bills, and how we judge that paying the bills is actually important. Conscious thought is what gives rise to language and expression, which are critical in connecting to the rest of the human family. Conscious thought makes it possible to achieve our noblest victories, and to feel the sting of our defeats. In the brain, this conscious ability is demarcated by what goes on in the primitive and subcortical structures (the brainstem, the limbic system) as opposed to what goes on in the cerebral cortex, the thin, outermost layer of the brain, the layer that makes humans truly unique from the rest of the animal kingdom. Here, in the cerebral cortex, is the center for all judgment, reasoning, rational thought, language and expression, impulse control, and the capacity to make and achieve long-term goals.

However, when the right frontal lobe is injured by stroke, trauma, or a tumor, the left brain does not have the capacity to take over critical cognition functions. This has led some within the field of neuroscience to call the area in and around the right frontal lobe the brain's "governing center."

Damage to this governing center can have curious results. If the junction between the right frontal, parietal, and temporal lobes is damaged by a stroke, judgment, intentional goal-oriented behavior, insight, self-awareness, and impulse control will be affected. It's as if the conscious mind gets untethered from the subconscious mind, leaving the subconscious mind to act and behave in an unchecked manner. Patients in this situation behave much like a jack-in-the-box toy, being wound up to surprisingly emerge, uncontrollably, with little ability to contain behaviors, actions, or comments. Family and friends of these people are often confused at this behavior, and left wondering how best to interact with the stroke patient. This is the typical area of damage in right middle cerebral stroke, one of the most common types of stroke. Damage to this area can cause potentially dangerous changes in behavior because of a lack of impulse control and judgment, sometimes leading to harming self and others. It can disrupt or diminish a person's capacity to avoid falls and injury and lead to a pattern of unwise decisions.

Furthermore, patients with right brain stroke syndromes may speak well so their actual abilities are often overestimated by others. These patients tend to have a lack of insight into their own deficits, while at the same time they have poor emotional control and do not display the normal emotional and social cues, leading others around them to have a confusing picture of their disorganized behavior. These stroke survivors are often impulsive and lack normal judgment for their actions, which sometimes leads to accidents or injuries.

When a Stroke Damages the Governing Center

To illustrate this undesirable behavior, let's look at how it manifests itself. Jen is a thirty-four-year-old mother who became addicted to heroin years ago. When I saw her as a patient, her intravenous drug use had caused an infection on her heart valve. The infection caused a clot to form that went up to her brain and caused a small stroke. Unfortunately, this stroke was exactly in the worst place in her situation: her governing center. Her stroke led to an alarming pattern of behavior defined by her lack of judgment, inappropriate comments, and a fixation on getting drugs to shoot through her accessible intravenous line, which we needed to use for her antibiotics. She referred to her IV line as a constant trigger due to the easy access to shoot up.

To solve the problems this behavior was causing, we had a medical team and family conference, as we often do, which Jen attended. In this conference, I saw two distressed parents who obviously loved their daughter, but they had already been through a lot on Jen's behalf. Jen, on the other hand, was placid and docile throughout the conference, with no evident ill intent or malice. She talked of wanting to inject heroin into her IV line just as casually and benignly as if she were asking for a drink of water. She said this many times, fixating on that one thought, even though IV drug use was what had gotten her into this situation in the first place. She didn't have the capacity to understand that if she did this, she could die. A four-year-old with a bottle of bubblegum-flavored poison would have been safer to herself. Jen's stroke had knocked out the governing center that controlled her insight into her situation, her ability to understand that actions have consequences, and her planning capability. It would be wrong to discount her prior pattern of behavior in leading to this difficult situation, but, clearly, the stroke affected her judgment, her impulse control, and her ability to make rational decisions.

Any filters Jen had previously possessed were now significantly diminished, if not completely shut off. It's as if all the subconscious thoughts and patterns now had access to the surface; if she had an inappropriate thought, she expressed it; if she had an impulse, she acted on it. She no longer had the capacity to filter her unconscious thoughts or rationally think through the consequences of her actions.

So much happens in our subconscious brain that is beneath the bright light of conscious thought: impulses, some of which may be protective, but can also be self-destructive; patterns or habits that are difficult to break; and biases that affect our actions and behaviors. We can't ignore that we have a subconscious brain, an unseen brain, out of conscious view. We can, however, make adjustments and adaptations as individuals and as families, to successfully accommodate these errors in thinking and judgment.

Neurological Neglect

Neurological neglect, also simply called neglect, is a subtle but extremely important clinical finding with many cases of stroke, especially the right-sided (right brain) stroke. Neurological neglect is defined as a failure to report, respond, or orient to sensory stimuli presented to the side opposite to the stroke side of the brain. It can result in such situations as bumping into things, tripping over things, ignoring food on one side of a plate, or grooming only one side of the body.

Although neglect can happen to both sides of the brain, neglect is much more common in patients with right-brain strokes (42 percent) than left-sided lesions (8 percent) and is more persistent in duration with right-sided strokes.[1] This is because damage to the right side of the brain leaves the left side to take over, and the left brain does not have the capacity to compensate for the loss of critical cognition functions in the right brain. In contrast, when the left side of the brain is damaged, the right frontal lobe can take over for both. So, why is the presence of neglect so important? One reason neglect is such an important stroke marker is that it is a powerful long-term indicator of patients' ability to achieve independence in their lives. Life independence is roughly defined as being able to manage personal affairs while living alone. The presence of neglect often requires family members to set up intermittent supervision for the patient, at the least, with someone checking in on the patient throughout the day.

More subtle forms of neglect are more common and more apparent during high levels of activity such as driving, working, or interacting with others. However, clinicians and scientists are currently making strides in models of predicting recovery using advanced imaging of the brain, and also methods of stimulating the brain in the early phase of recovery to ascertain what brain processes still exist—the processes that are initially stunned but can recover with time. What can be said with confidence is that when neurological neglect resolves, patients do much better and have many more options in terms of life skills such as driving, working, living safely alone, and recreating. Milder neglect involves various degrees of ignoring the affected side when faced with stimulation on the unaffected side. Again, the importance of this subtle but significant finding after stroke cannot be underscored enough; neglect can cause substantial impairments and burdens to both the patient and family members or caregivers.

The President Who Forgot How to Govern

An interesting case-in-point is the Woodrow Wilson Presidency. In 1919, President Wilson, while debating a bill on the Senate floor, suddenly collapsed with weakness on the left side of his body due to a stroke. For such a bright president—the first to have a PhD, a president of Princeton College, an academician, and a Nobel Peace Prize winner—this cognition impairment of his governing center was a serious blow. Without the advantages of advanced imaging, we are left to assume by his reported symptoms that the stroke hit his right middle cerebral artery territory, with symptoms of left-sided weakness, and a neurological neglect syndrome. Thus, he ignored things and people on the left side of his body, often running into objects or people. This syndrome of neglect is almost universally accompanied by *executive function* deficits. Executive function refers to a person's attention, their ability to focus on short-term and long-term goals, and their planning how to achieve those goals. The presence of left neglect, we now know, reflects poorly for the patient's cognitive function, especially important for a sitting president of the United States.

President Wilson was treated at the hospital for a stroke that paralyzed his left arm and leg. After weeks receiving medical and therapeutic care, a delegation of doctors and senators came to assess whether he was fit to govern, since the Senate has the responsibility to make this judgment whenever a president has a major health crisis. The First Lady, Edith Bolling Wilson, noticed that President Wilson had an extremely difficult time attending to things and people positioned on the left side of his body. Therefore, she positioned his chair with his left side facing a wall, and arranged the delegation of senators and doctors on his right side so he could pay attention to his guests better. President Wilson talked about current and past events, laughed with the delegation, and impressed the doctors and senators so much that they concluded he was still "fit to govern." Although President Wilson would serve for two more years, until the end of his term, we now know that the First Lady was required to make all long-term decisions about strategy for her husband—he simply could not pay attention long enough to process important decisions. His cognitive impairment seems to have remained until his death in 1924.[2] That this severe cognitive impairment was not readily recognized by the best doctors of the day and his colleagues in the Senate, but was very apparent to the people living with him, teaches an important lesson even today. The right-brain neglect cognitive syndrome is subtle but significant, and sometimes requires some degree of long-term caregiving and supervision to manage the patient's affairs. Resolution of neurological neglect syndrome appears to be an important marker of recovery, which sometimes occurs, sometimes not.

Our Understanding of Neurological Neglect Syndrome Today

The deficits that occur in neurological neglect syndrome (usually due to a right brain stroke) are better-known, treated, and many times alleviated, but deficits from this syndrome usually do not completely resolve. A woman named Barbara had this same type of stroke in her late forties with neurological neglect syndrome and weakness on her left side. On the day of the stroke, Barbara woke and was unable to move her left side, arm, and leg. She was transported to a hospital, where she was diagnosed with a right middle cerebral artery stroke.

But Barbara's recovery proved to be slow, through an inpatient rehabilitation center and, eventually, she was transferred to a skilled nursing facility for the further work her neurological neglect syndrome deficits required. She finally gained enough independence to move into an apartment with her son, even though her son worked during the day, leaving her home alone. She worked hard with the home health therapists who came to her home, and then she went to our outpatient therapy clinic, which specializes in stroke neuro-rehabilitation. At the specialty clinic, she took and passed a driver's test, despite her history of neurological neglect syndrome. She now drives without restrictions and without difficulty, further enhancing her independence. She often gets lost, however, due to a right-brain syndrome deficit leading to deficits in "path-finding," or an individual's spatial orientation and recognition (i.e., they don't know where they are, where they are going, and can't visualize the pathway to the destination). Barbara is able to accommodate for this deficit by using a GPS unit when she drives. She also has learned to accommodate for some executive function deficits by use of a simple notebook in which she writes down appointments, etc. She lives alone in an apartment now, is active in a health and wellness program, and travels extensively with her two sons, who provide her with encouragement and assistance for high-level cognition tasks. Recently, Barbara has been volunteering at the local hospital where she first received medical care, thereby giving back to the community, creating valuable social connections, and further enhancing her quality of life. That's not to say her life is perfect—she still walks with a cane, battles stiff, tight muscles on her left side, and is on an antidepressant; however, she tells me, "You've got to make the most of your life," and that's what she is doing.

Summary

To understand the cognitive effects after a stroke, one has to understand the difference between the subconscious and conscious brain. When stroke damages the coupling structures within the brain, it can lead to changes in behavior, especially if the governing center is damaged.

This damage can lead to neurological changes in behavior, such as neglect and deficits in executive function. These deficits are often subtle, but they are significant both to the stroke survivor and their family and friends. It sometimes takes significant adjustment and adaptation, but a high quality of life can still be achieved.

CHAPTER 12

DESPITE CHANCE EVENTS, YOU CAN MAKE YOUR MARK

Success means doing the best we can with what we have. Success is the doing, not the getting—in the trying, not the triumph. Success is a personal standard, reaching for the highest that is in us, becoming all that we can be.

— Zig Ziglar

Where a stroke lands, with its specific effects on the brain, may be quite random, like a message in a bottle carried by the ocean's tides. Also, certain elements in an individual's body may make stroke more likely. Some of these factors are easily discoverable, while others are not usually discovered until you have a stroke. These predisposing factors may be related to common genetic factors (clotting disorders, the way your body processes cholesterol, etc.), but there are also frequent anomalies and variants relating to the way our blood vessels are formed before we are born.

Although stroke can have devastating impacts, some less obvious, though still significant, effects of stroke also exist. This chapter will outline some of the many anatomic variants that sometimes lead to stroke, some less apparent effects of stroke, approaches to treatment, accommodation of these effects, and how to retain a healthy and productive quality of life.

Anatomical Varieties: The Artery of Percheron's Peculiar Consequence

All people are not built the same. Our outward characteristics make this obvious, but it is equally true for our bodies' inner workings. We are even different in our vasculature—how we are "plumbed" for delivery of blood to the organs, including the brain. Some of these variations can predispose different people to different health problems. Here's one important example: About one-quarter of humans have a variant left over from being in the womb, receiving their mothers' oxygenated blood. Every fetus has a hole in its heart that allows the already-oxygen-rich blood from the mother to bypass the infant's lungs while still in the womb. When the infant takes its first breath, that hole normally begins to close. However, in about 25 percent of people, that hole, called a patent foramen ovale, never closes. Most people live their whole lives never realizing they have this anatomical variant, nor should they be concerned. However, in rare cases, a blood clot originating from another part of the body can pass through that hole, bypassing the lungs, and make its way up the neck to the brain and cause a stroke.

The brain itself has variants in its plumbing. For example, another important situation is a little known variant in the plumbing of the brain called the artery of Percheron. This artery is present in about one-third of all people, and is, unfortunately, a factor in a rare but disabling stroke of the brain structure called the thalamus, which is deep in the brain on both sides. The interesting thing is that a clot in the artery of Percheron will produce a stroke in both sides of the brain, but only in the thalamus. Though this stroke syndrome is rare, the pumping problems that predispose people for this type of stroke are present in 100 million Americans, making it too common and yet costly to screen for. Also, if discovered, it would be too risky and costly to try to rearrange the brain's plumbing, so nothing can be done.

Such was the case with a young medical resident I saw who had strokes on both sides of his brain due to a single clot on the artery of Percheron. Strokes of this type usually cause problems with the regulation of consciousness and alertness, causing difficulty in maintaining attention. In the initial stages, it is usually difficult to get these patients to wake up for even brief periods, to talk (even though their language skills are intact), or to participate in therapy.

This resident's long-term goal was to graduate from his medical residency program. We worked together rigorously on that goal for a couple of years, but ultimately, he wasn't ready to take the necessary board exams, owing to his strange and subtle cognitive deficits. He did, however, secure a nice position as a researcher; he also got married and now has two kids. Life goes on for this man, and he and his new wife are making the most of their lives. He still has much to give to his family and society in general. He is making his mark by being the best husband and father he can be, and through his research, he will bless many lives.

Ataxia: The Sometimes Poorly Recognized Deficit

The weakness and numbness that occur with most stroke syndromes is very apparent to outsiders and thus easy to understand. However, *ataxia* is another common effect of some forms of stroke; it has significant and disabling effects that may not be immediately recognized by outside observers. Usually, ataxia is caused by a stroke in the cerebellum, a structure in the back of the brain, with its blood supply coming from the vertebral artery. The cerebellum controls coordination and fine movements, such as handwriting or picking up small items, and usually only affects one side of the body. Thus, ataxic patients have problems with coordination and balance. These problems often lead to dizziness (vertigo), which then leads to nausea, which is sometimes severe. Often, patients have nausea and vomiting every time they move their heads, which is a real barrier to therapeutic activities. A stroke in the cerebellum doesn't affect strength, but this incoordination (ataxia) and balance issues often lead to problems with walking and frequent falls.

However, patients with cerebellar stroke retain their cognitive skills.

Generally, they can return to work and participate in many common leisure activities, with or without accommodations such as a cane or walker.

Such was the case with Dr. Peters, a successful obstetrician in his early forties. Having a stroke was quite a shock for this otherwise healthy young doctor. The stroke hit one side of his cerebellum, causing severe motor incoordination (ataxia) and vertigo, along with poor balance and intractable nausea. We treated the nausea with a cocktail of three anti-nausea medications, which finally enabled him to participate in therapy. His ataxia and balance deficits improved to the point where he could walk with a cane—carefully and slowly, but he could do it alone. We sent him home to his rural community, where he was determined to continue therapy and continue improving. He, too, had the long-term goal of returning to work as a doctor and surgeon, which was a reasonable goal, especially since the cerebellar stroke hadn't affected his cognition, although motor information on one side was a formidable obstacle for a surgeon. The nausea eventually improved. He began going in to his office, then hired another partner to help serve his patients. With time, he began to see patients in the outpatient clinic. He began assisting his new partner in the operating room. His recovery of function continued. He eventually prevailed and now is back to being a fully competent and successful doctor. His path to recovery was not easy nor short, and he had to make some significant concessions and adjustments. However, he showed remarkable resilience and fortitude—and his efforts paid off. He is continuing to make his mark.

Locked-In Syndrome

The basilar artery is another artery that supplies the brainstem with blood. When a clot or hemorrhage occurs in the basilar artery, a condition called locked-in syndrome can ensue. Locked-in syndrome is truly devastating, as demonstrated by one courageous man, Jean-Dominique Bauby, who was the editor-in-chief of the French *Elle* magazine. He suffered a stroke of the basilar artery and lapsed into a coma. He awoke twenty days later, mentally aware of his surroundings, but physically paralyzed, with complete lack of ability to move any muscle, except for some movement in his head and eyes. The stroke took away his ability to breathe, so he required mechanical ventilation. Also, his ability to swallow was gone, so he required nutrition from a feeding tube placed in his stomach. His right eye had to be sewn shut due to an irrigation problem. Incredibly, he was able to write an entire book, *The Diving Bell and the Butterfly*, which took him ten months, by simply blinking his left eyelid, as someone trained in a complex and elegant system transcribed the eye-blinks into letters and words. In his book, the diving bell represents his flaccid body, and the butterfly represents his active mind. In a true testament to the power of the human spirit, Bauby details how, even with extremely limited abilities, he can still have rich experiences in his mind, and vivid memories. He expresses such emotions, plus his sorrow at seeing his children but being unable to touch them and his disappointment when he doesn't pass his dietary test because then he has to "eat" through a tube connected to his stomach. His only taste of food is in his memories, where he imagines himself cooking dishes. He concludes the book with a thought: "Does the cosmos contain keys for opening up my diving bell? A subway line with no terminus? A currency strong enough to buy my freedom back? We must keep looking. I'll be off now."[1] On March 9, 1997, two days after his book was published, Bauby died of pneumonia, but his words, testifying to the power of the human spirit, live on. He continues to make his mark.

Wallenberg's Syndrome

The signs of some stroke syndromes make up a collection of ambiguous, minor symptoms, but having to deal with the aggregate of these many difficulties can be quite disabling. Furthermore, for patients who receive little or no education about these symptoms, which are normal and to be expected, it can be an emotionally confusing and vexing problem. Such is the case with Wallenberg's syndrome.

The other day in my outpatient clinic, I saw a man in emotional distress. He'd had a stroke a couple of years ago that was diagnosed as a cerebellar stroke. Indeed, the main syndrome fits the diagnosis: ataxia, incoordination of one side, problems with balance, and vertigo, leading to nausea. But those symptoms almost completely resolved over the course of six months. However, my patient began noticing a constellation of vague and indistinct symptoms, none of which was severe, but they made him wonder if he was going out of his mind. He reported dryness in one eye and a lack of feeling, specifically to temperature and sharp pain, on one side of his body and on the opposite side of his face. He was bothered by his voice being slightly hoarse. He was disturbed by a sense of "not normal" coordination, though ever so slight. Also, when he would work out, his face would just sweat on one side.

It turns out he had two locations of strokes, at the same time, in similar areas, with some similar traits, but other traits were distinctly different. His symptoms from the cerebellar stroke had resolved, but not the symptoms from the lateral medulla stroke, which produced Wallenberg's syndrome.

Wallenberg's syndrome produces about ten or twelve neurologic symptoms. Many of them can be so mild and faint that patients do not even realize they have them until weeks or sometimes months after the stroke. In the setting of stroke that produces one or two severe deficits, most people have to spend all their mental and physical energy addressing the acute problems they face. Eventually, the acute problems improve, and, especially in the case of Wallenberg's syndrome, the patients start to notice other strange neurologic features. For example, typical Wallenberg's syndrome features include ataxia, vertigo, and swallowing problems (major features that patients notice right away), but also a slightly droopy upper eyelid on one side, unequal pupil size, one dry eye, lack of sweat over one-half of the face, decreased sensation over one-half of the face and the opposite side of the body, a hoarse voice, and hiccups.

Perhaps more important to this man is that he had, in the two years since his stroke, never heard of Wallenberg's syndrome, nor been educated on the strange symptoms he was experiencing. He explained that his symptoms, none of which were severe, when added together made him feel like "I am dying by a thousand papercuts." He had been on a maladaptive spiral, partially because he was in the dark for so long—lacking the proper education about his unique syndrome. Information is important, so he was very relieved that this syndrome had a name. Now armed with this information and the support of others in his support network, hopefully, he can turn this situation around and get on an adaptive spiral. He has vast potential to get on the right track and eventually make a mark on society.

Summary

Some factors are out of anyone's control. These factors pertain to the way the brain is plumbed to receive blood, and they are completely left to chance. In this life, you can assume the role of the hunter or the prey. Despite stroke, you can still make your mark on this world, even if it means communicating by blinking one eye. The human spirit cannot be broken…unless you let it break. You can stay on the adaptive spiral. You can have a good, if not great, quality of life.

CHAPTER 13

SURROUNDING YOURSELF WITH GREAT RESOURCES: CRITICAL COLLABORATIONS

Harmony and strength exist in our lives only when [there is] harmony between our deepest and purest yearning and the goals we pursue in life.

— Albert Schweitzer

This chapter is about amassing all the resources available. Struggles will invariably ensue and you will need all the help you can get. With a stroke, the human body is torn down to its weakest elements and the human brain fails on a grand scale. Initially, the physical and psychological discord and friction are overpowering. But then, through tremendous personal effort, one can build up a portion of the body, learn to adapt, pick up the pieces, and struggle to regain some semblance of a normal life. This process may take a long time. This is the process of recovery.

There are certain critical things for you to do along the way—things only you can do. Conversely, there are certain critical things for others to do to assist you—things your rehabilitation team, family, and friends do. It is crucial for you to accept their help, guidance, and assistance.

In a sense, this is a time for both collaboration with your own mind and collaboration with others. Stephen R. Covey explains this as being *interdependent*, as opposed to being fully independent, which you may have been before your stroke, as most men and women are. Being interdependent in critical relationships with your rehabilitation team, your family, and your friends, says Covey, "will require the exercise of unique human endowment of self-awareness, imagination, consciousness, and independent will.... It involves mutual learning, mutual influence, and mutual benefits."[1] This is a time for alignment of priorities within your own mind and amassing resources to assist you along the way. In this way, you can act synergistically, which means simply that the value of the sum becomes greater than the value of the parts alone, working toward a common goal. Usually, this goal is for successful preparation to go home and get on with the things that matter most to you.

The Foundation to Thrive

In his book *What Doesn't Kill You: The New Psychology of Posttraumatic Growth*, Stephen Joseph poses a very helpful acronym to help individuals develop resilience in the face of struggles and trials: THRIVE. Here is how it breaks down:

- **Taking Stock:** Make a mental picture of all the personal attributes and characteristics you possess. You are going to need to draw upon all your strengths, but first you have to identify them. For example, one might identify a history of being physically fit, and the training and endurance will greatly aid you as you work to regain strength. In my case, I identified that I had learned a foreign language, Japanese, as a young man. As I regained language capacity, relearning how to form all the sounds of the English language, I remembered the difficulty and struggle, but also the sense of accomplishment I had already achieved in learning Japanese.

- **Harvesting Hope:** Look to the future by setting short, intermediate, and long-term goals. Be realistic, but hopeful, in your plans for the future. If you can, write them down. For me and many other stroke patients, it was a few weeks before I could even write the simplest thoughts. I had the goal, written down in a spiral-bound notebook, of being able to walk without a cane. For others, the goal may be feeding yourself with your weak hand and arm. It could be anything since most stroke patients have countless skills to remaster. I believe it's important to write your goals down—unwritten, a goal is merely a wish.

- **Re-Authoring:** Change from a victim mindset to a survivor mindset and then, eventually, to a thriving mindset as you take steps toward an adaptive spiral. Don't be afraid to take baby steps. Have courage when you think you look silly in your valiant attempts in therapy and on your own. The second element of the adaptive spiral is "Exploration." Don't be afraid to explore your new situation—the changes in your body and your interactions with the environment surrounding you. You are the hunter, not the prey, which is often difficult to remember when you are struggling to do simple tasks like walking without stumbling or speaking in simple and understandable words. Yet it is true.

- **Identifying Change:** Track your progress and growth. The changes in your brain will be imperceptible to you if you don't keep track of them. Keep track of your progress on a daily basis of the distance walked, of the amount of assistance needed, and eventually, of the speed at which you can do the activities that once were such a struggle. Tracking progress is an intrinsic motivating factor. In most stroke recovery cases, there will be positive progress on a daily basis, in the first stages of recovery.

- **Valuing Change:** Develop a sense of gratitude for the changes you have adapted to. It's hard to imagine in the early stages after stroke, but you may come to value the struggles and how they have led to growth and improvement. Remember, a large part of this recovery process will be dependent on your ability to embrace change and adaptation.

- **Expressing Change in Action:** Make choices to align your growth into everyday behaviors and attitudes. Here is where the adaptive spiral becomes a habit. Dedicate one or two hours per day to focused efforts in recovery. For example, each morning I spent twenty minutes practicing correctly forming some basic sounds. Then, I progressed to twenty minutes per day of reading children's books aloud, while focusing on correctly forming the words, then reading adult literature aloud. I eventually began listening to radio announcers' dialogue; then, sentence by sentence, I turned the radio down and practiced imitating the dialogue. (Some have joked that I learned many expressions from National Public Radio [NPR] announcers.) This principle of change can be put into action in countless ways.[2]

Following the six THRIVE approaches will help prepare your mind for the task ahead.

Understand Rehabilitation Triage

Several rehabilitative environments (settings to receive rehabilitation) exist; screening assessments for the ideal rehabilitative environment should be performed as soon as possible. Typically, the rehabilitation environment should fit the patient's current function status. For example, patients with mild deficits after stroke and a high functional status can go home and receive outpatient therapy or home health therapy and assistance. For more moderate to severe deficits, the environment of inpatient rehabilitation may be preferred; however, patients deemed eligible for an inpatient rehabilitation program must be able to *learn* and have *sufficient endurance* to participate. The most powerful predictor of rehabilitation outcomes is initial stroke severity, followed by age.

Initially, your eligibility to receive therapy in any rehabilitative environment may depend on your ability to participate in effortful guided therapy. Younger patients account for a smaller percentage of individuals with stroke. These patients typically do well with rehabilitation, making significant functional gains, and nearly all are discharged home. In general, all eligible patients should be engaged in rehabilitation as soon as able.

Elderly patients with stroke should be considered for their potential as candidates for medical and rehabilitation training at an inpatient rehabilitation facility if they can participate in meaningful therapy, regardless of stroke severity. This is, in part, due to elderly patients having other complex medical issues requiring more intense medical monitoring. Nonetheless, each case needs to be considered on the basis of individual characteristics and potential. Factors such as premorbid fitness, cognitive functioning, family/community support, and other medical problems besides stroke are important to consider when making decisions about stroke affecting your elderly loved one.

Whenever possible, based on best evidence, patients with moderate to severe strokes should receive rehabilitation on stroke-specific rehabilitation units, given their usual complex medical and rehabilitation needs.

When starting a rehabilitation program, it is important that you, as a patient, and your family, begin with the proper mindset. Neuro-rehabilitation does not happen quickly. Don't get frustrated, especially with the rehabilitation team trying to guide you. It's a marathon, not a sprint. Your therapy team will accept you without conditions—hopefully, you will feel safe, secure, validated, and affirmed in your essential worth, identity, and integrity.

Two sides to the coin exist when it comes to stroke recovery. The vast majority of stroke patients are faced with challenges that need to be overcome in respect to both sides of the recovery coin. On the one side, you will be working intently on what is best described as **neurologic restoration**. Neurologic restoration means the function is restored to the pre-stroke level, whether it is the arm, hand, or leg function; speech abilities; etc. Your rehabilitation team will have methods to facilitate that restoration to your maximal potential. The other side of the coin is best described as **func-**

tional adaptive compensation. Functional adaptation means the person is taught methods to adapt, *despite impairments that remain*, to further maximize their potential for a high-functioning life.

Current efforts are underway to help better identify the potential for neurologic restoration within the first week after stroke. Simple clinical tests done at the bedside are being developed, along with more sophisticated, though equally harmless, techniques such as using magnetic stimulation to check whether a neurologic signal can traverse the brain circuitry to the arm or leg, or using special MRIs to detect if a person still has the critical brain circuitry to communicate with the arm or leg. Sometimes, the damage from the stroke is such that a signal cannot get through, so the brain cannot "speak" to the arm or leg and, thus, does not have the future potential for meaningful use of the affected limb. For people in this situation, this loss is a sad part of the aftermath of stroke. I personally went through this loss. However, what is not neurologically restored can usually be adequately adapted for in a functional way. In this way, especially in the future, neurology and rehabilitation teams can better tailor patients' rehabilitation efforts to the functional adaption side of the coin, rather than just spinning the wheels of neurologic restoration. Plenty can be done on both sides of the coin. Again, the overarching goal is to facilitate the highest quality of life possible, and that requires a lot of effort on both sides of the coin.

It's important to have a general framework that will be guiding the professional, who will then guide your rehabilitation course. However, the first responsibility lies within yourself…to get up on your feet and try, day in and day out. Everything should get steadily better if you make the effort.

The Four Horsemen

It is of paramount importance that your rehabilitation team work behind the scenes to prepare you for the intensity and rigors of recovery and rehabilitative activities. That is not to say they should go behind your or your family's back. Rather, they should be setting the stage for your success, while you and your family may still be reeling from the shock of it all. Any decisions should still be made in consultation with you and your family. The rehabilitation team just presents options for you to decide upon.

Four factors are critically important to address in your recovery in the initial stages of rehabilitation activities. They are so important to your rehab efforts that I have begun referring to them as the Four Horsemen. If the Four Horsemen factors aren't addressed, the horses will be compromised right out of their starting gates, leading to increased chances of fail-points in your recovery efforts. The Four Horsemen are: poor arousal, poor mood, pain, and poor motivation/despondency.

Poor arousal is a factor in many strokes. For reasons too complex for this book, the physiological response after stroke, among the host of other deficits, is drowsiness, trouble staying awake, and problems attending to tasks and therapy. The hard work of recovery can't begin when the stroke patient is sleeping much of the day. Because stroke recovery is a very active process, you literally get back only what you intently work at through your own efforts, usually guided by therapists, and you can't really begin that process unless you are fully awake and alert.

Your quality of sleep at night should be optimized. This is called sleep-wake cycle hygiene. The medical team may prescribe a neuro-stimulant to be taken in the morning for a time. This medication is generally safe for stroke patients and is usually well tolerated. This medication's goal is active participation in therapy activities.

Poor mood is also a problem for many stroke patients. A stroke is psychologically traumatic for the patient and their family. Furthermore, a stroke can exacerbate an ongoing problem of depression or anxiety. The patient may feel overwhelmed—sometimes this leads to adjustment disorder. The presence of depression in the first year after a stroke is about 25 percent higher than in the general population, but the situation of "the sky is falling" is not the scenario for most people.

Nevertheless, mood should be treated aggressively. Support and encouragement should be given by all the rehabilitation team, and, as much as possible, by family and friends. Supportive counseling by the rehabilitation psychologist is also helpful.

Pain is sometimes an inhibiting factor for participation in therapeutic activities. Most of the time when people have problems with pain, their pain has been a chronic issue, since stroke usually doesn't cause pain. Chronic low back, hip, or knee pain that has been present for a long time is usual. However, patients are typically not very motivated to expend a full effort in therapy when doing so causes significant amounts of pain. The goal is not to eliminate 100 percent of pain with strong opiate medications, but to reduce the pain enough that meaningful therapy can take place. Sometimes conservative methods, such as ice or over-the-counter pain medications, are adequate. Still, other patients require more potent pain medications; the potency should be minimal, though sufficient to allow full participation in therapeutic activities.

Some pain syndromes are specific to stroke, but these syndromes typically occur a couple of weeks to a few months after a stroke. Some examples are hemiplegic shoulder pain and neuropathic pain syndrome, both of which are addressed in Chapter 14.

Poor motivation and despondency are sometimes present after a stroke. At times, people give up, feeling no reason left to try. Poor motivation and depression frequently go hand-in-hand. Education about stroke recovery is helpful because the situation is often not as bleak as one might think. People do recover function and go on to live meaningful lives. A peer mentor coming to see the patient is often a good idea.

One rare neurological syndrome, however, called abulia, does affect a person's motivation. Patients with abulia have an apathetic attitude about most things—they are not depressed; they just don't give a full effort in therapy because they don't care that much, which is a difficult situation to be in. Nevertheless, the rehabilitation environment and encouraging rehabilitation therapists and staff seem to make a big difference because the culture is geared toward achieving positive results.

Climbing the Ladder

For most stroke patients, recovery will demand effective goal setting to overcome barriers and the obstacles of hemiplegia and sensory loss, language deficits, cognitive problems, and sometimes pain, depression, and spasticity. Again, to be most effective, optimal goal setting should be a collaborative effort between the patient, physician, and therapy staff. Overcoming the deficits brought on by stroke is usually a long, laborious process, but by working together, goal by goal, step by step, significant results and higher satisfaction and quality of life can ensue.

Successfully treating a stroke is like climbing a ladder. Basic skills must be conquered before climbing to the next rung. For this reason, treatment can be thought of as being carried out in cycles. Optimally, every treatment cycle has four components.

1. **Clinical Assessment:** Each cycle should begin with a clinical assessment with you, your rehabilitation doctor, and possibly a therapist. The clinical assessment is where you identify strengths and weaknesses.

2. **Goal Setting:** Armed with the information from the clinical assessment, you will be ready to explore appropriate goals. This exploration crosses over to the personal adaptive spiral since exploring the possibilities for your life and goal setting are common to both cycles. Again, appropriate goal setting involves the patient, the physician, and the therapists. Working in this coordinated manner with a physician and therapists, you can set realistic goals that will have a positive impact on your progression. The physician can coordinate medical interventions, if needed, and the therapy team can put in place activities that will support specific goals.

3. **Functional Progress:** Hard work and guidance from the rehabilitation team will lead to functional progress. Persistence is key to this process.

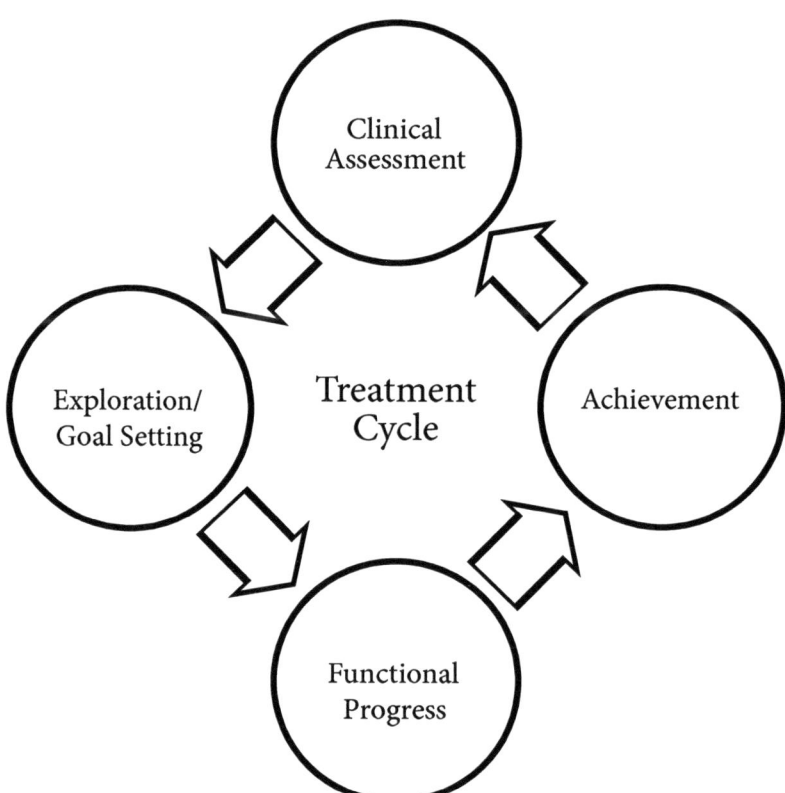

Collaborative Victory

4. **Achievement:** When goals are reached or sufficient progress has been made, you deserve to recognize your achievements. Achievements in the treatment cycle may be objective clinical measures, like walking faster on a timed walking test, or they may be functional tasks that you can now do on your own.

At the end of the cycle, you should be reassessed by your rehabilitation doctor and therapy staff. Then the cycle starts over again. In this way, your entire rehabilitation team can take part in the adaptive spiral.

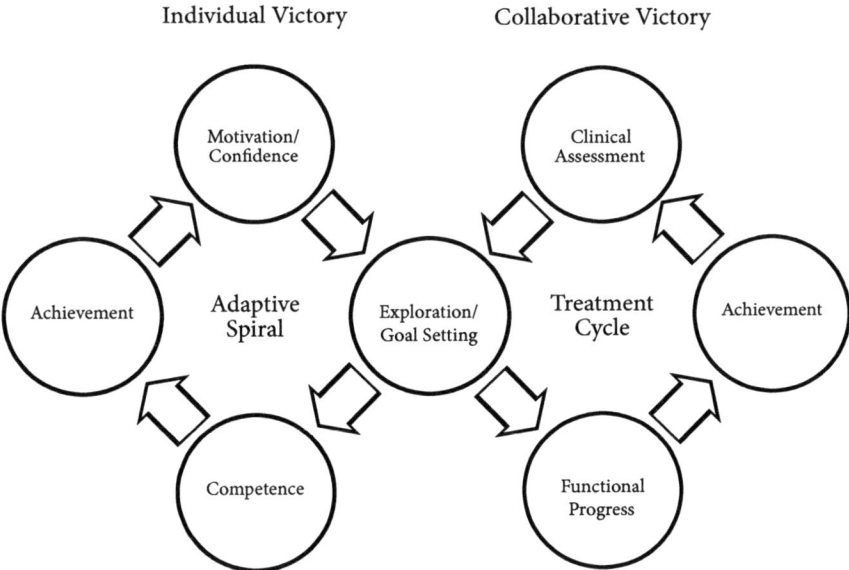

Summary

Stroke patients face enormous challenges in recovering lost skills, finding meaningful ways to engage in the world, and learning to navigate physically at home and in their communities. It is of critical importance to embrace the interdependent collaboration between yourself and the rehabilitation team; this may be one of the most important aspects of your recovery process. You must have resilience and work hard, with directions and guidance from the rehabilitation team. The rehabilitation team will, in turn, be watching and addressing common factors that can become barriers. Ultimate success may take months and even years to achieve, and it will depend on interdependent relationships guiding you through the adaptive spiral, leading to greater satisfaction and a higher quality of life.

CHAPTER 14

COMPLICATIONS AFTER A STROKE: GORILLAS AND FROGS

It's a little like wrestling a gorilla. You don't quit when you're tired—you quit when the gorilla is tired.

— Robert Strauss

In the aftermath of your stroke, there may be many changes, small and large. Some changes will be a natural consequence of the stroke's effects on your body. You should be aware of the early and late changes to your body. You will also be more susceptible to some common complications after stroke. You should know how to avoid these complications and what to do if they occur. At times, you may feel like you are holding back the tide with a broom, but in this case, knowledge is power. Good treatment options generally exist for both the later expected consequences and the complications of stroke.

I like to think of stroke complications by using two metaphors. We all can conceive of a gorilla, the big 400-pound type. Most of us have seen gorillas at the zoo, behind bars. Now imagine that the 400-pound gorilla escaped from the zoo. "Gorilla on the loose" dominates the local media; TV and radio reports abound. Everyone would be aware, vigilant, and cautious—everyone except those who missed the news report, don't watch TV, or don't listen to the radio. If the gorilla on the loose was sighted by someone who had no idea that seeing a gorilla was even a possibility, it would likely be much more frightening than for someone who had heard the news reports and was vigilantly watching. That is the way some complications are after a stroke: You want to be aware of the risks and be cautious and vigilant; otherwise, they might catch you off-guard, and be much more frightening and possibly even deadly. Delay in recognition and treatment could cause major setbacks in your recovery process. This chapter will educate you on the gorillas you may encounter and help you avoid setbacks.

My other metaphor for stroke complications is a frog in hot water. Some of the complications after stroke can be much more insidious in onset. They say if you heat water up to a boil and then toss a frog in, the frog will just jump out unscathed. However, if you set the frog in the pot with the water at room temperature, and then slowly raise the temperature, the frog will calmly swim around the pot, being imperceptible to the rising temperature. When the temperature becomes dangerously high, the poor frog will get scalded and possibly die. In a stroke's aftermath, the slow insidious development of some fairly common factors can lead to regressions in your physical abilities. This often leads to decompensation to the maladaptive spiral.

I will base management of stroke complications on these two metaphors to help conceptualize.

Gorillas in Our Midst

If one of these gorillas does come within your view, even comes to visit you for a time, it is important to know that the possibility of gorillas does exist so you are not so frightened nor caught off-guard. Following are some of the various problems that can arise after stroke. Further neurological complications, although not likely, can present themselves in a stroke's aftermath. They include:

- **Swallowing problems:** Also known as dysphagia, swallowing problems are common after stroke.

- **Aspiration:** Swallowing food or liquid down the "wrong pipe" (the trachea that leads to the lung) is known as aspiration and can lead to a form of pneumonia called aspiration pneumonia. Silent aspiration means the stroke patient does not cough, gag, choke, or have any other outward signs of difficulty. Of patients who aspirate, up to 50 percent may be *silent aspirators*, so aspiration may go undetected until pneumonia sets in. Pneumonia is a leading cause of death within the first month after stroke. This can usually be prevented by adhering to the swallowing precaution set out by speech therapy.

- **Recurrent stroke:** Most people worry about having another stroke. While within thirty months the risk of having a recurrent stroke is about 10 percent, one has to take that figure within the context that the average age for stroke is around eighty years of age, and that stroke risk increases with age.

- **Hemorrhagic transformation:** Early after stroke, this neurological event is more likely than a second stroke. Hemorrhagic transformation is when the area of the brain damaged by an ischemic stroke begins to bleed into the brain. The results are usually quite vague because the bleed is mainly affecting the already-damaged brain cells.

- **Seizures:** Seizures are another complication that can occur after stroke, though the likelihood of seizures developing is only about 3 percent.

- **Deep venous thrombosis:** When paralysis of one or more body parts occurs, with the usual inactivity of the limb, your venous system is more likely to have pooling of blood in the veins of your limbs. With this stasis, sometimes clots form called deep venous thrombosis, an unlikely occurrence.

- **Pulmonary embolism:** If deep venous thrombosis occurs, then when the clots break off and travel through the bloodstream, they usually get caught in the lungs, which is called a pulmonary embolism. It is also rare, but may be life-threatening.

- **Urinary tract infection:** Infections, like bladder infections and IV line infections, are also common, though usually quite simple to treat. By far the most common form of infection is a urinary tract infection (UTI), or a bladder infection.

- **Falls:** With weakness and lack of coordination, falls sometimes occur. Special attention should be given to people known to be at high risk for a fall because of their cognitive deficits.

Perhaps 400-pound gorillas lurk in all of our lives. The challenge is to be aware of them, take the necessary precautions to keep ourselves safe, and not worry or ruminate on these things needlessly.

Keeping the Frog's Water Cool

We must also monitor the temperature of the water our frog is swimming in. To do that, we must know the factors that can lead to water with dangerously high temperatures and take the steps necessary to avoid excessive discomfort and difficulties. Below are the factors to be aware of because they can cause unique and unfamiliar problems that you may not perceive immediately, but they may turn into problems that require medical attention.

- **Central neuropathic pain** is one of the rather insidious factors that stroke patients commonly deal with. It refers to the pain sensation originating in the brain (central) without any injury to the skin or any other part of the body. This central neuropathic pain is sometimes referred to by names like thalamic pain syndrome or complex regional pain syndrome, but the problem with each of these is that the brain interprets normal everyday sensations as pain. Central neuropathic pain can feel like a numb, tingly sensation, like a wire brush being applied to the skin or, in extreme cases, broken glass rubbing on the skin. Needless to say, this can cause significant ongoing discomfort. Additionally, when one is focused intently on pain management, it takes attention off recovery efforts and may set the patient on the path to a maladaptive spiral. The onset of central neuropathic pain is late—most people who have this problem begin to feel mild sensory changes about two to four weeks after a stroke. But the pain often just increases as the "water gets hotter," until it consumes their thoughts and behavior. The good news is medications and methods exist for alleviating this pain. With several classes of non-opiate medications your doctor can recommend, the "edge" can be taken off, although the sensations don't typically go away entirely.

- **Hemiplegic shoulder pain** is another relatively common pain syndrome. It deals specifically with the shoulder on the weak hemiplegic side. Its frequency is significantly greater in patients who require inpatient rehabilitation (because their deficits tend to be worse), affecting about half of this segment of stroke survivors in the first six months. Because a painful shoulder causes patients to avoid using the hemiplegic arm, its occurrence can limit participation in rehabilitation activities and impair function, leading to a maladaptive spiral.

An understanding of the relationship between shoulder anatomy, hemiplegia, and the spastic states of the arm is often helpful in this complex problem. The shoulder and its surrounding muscles normally have protective responses, which are often impaired after a stroke, which can lead to such things as rotator cuff damage or shoulder impingement. Shoulder subluxation (dropping) is initially present because the whole shoulder girdle is weakened by the stroke. A few weeks later, as is often the case, spasticity develops and over-tightened muscles may further limit normal movement. This complex situation of hemiplegic shoulder pain is lumped into a whole array of conditions such as subluxation, spasticity, adhesive capsulitis, impingement syndromes, bursitis, rotator cuff tears, brachial plexus traction neuropathies, and complex regional pain syndrome.

Ideally, management should begin with careful efforts to prevent shoulder pain from occurring in the first place. Poor handling of the affected limb is thought to play a role in contributing to later shoulder pain. Care should be taken in transferring (from bed to chair, etc.) and handling the weak arm and shoulder. Treatment options include over-the-counter pain medications or nonsteroidal anti-inflammatory drugs (NSAIDs), which should be used initially, as their success and effectiveness have been well established. Joint injections with corticosteroids are also often successful in alleviating this type of shoulder pain. Also, neuromuscular electrical stimulation of the shoulder muscles, along with a stretching program, has been found to decrease pain and increase range of motion, and it may also facilitate use of the weak arm. Botulinum toxin injections to tight, spastic muscles may help if spasticity is present. Stretching and strengthening of the shoulder muscles, under the guidance of skilled therapists, is also recommended.

- **Spasticity and hypertonia** are also common complications of a stroke. (Chapter 16 will address these in-depth.) Basically, the muscles on the weak, hemiplegic side may start to get tight at around two to four weeks after a stroke. This, too, can have an insidious onset. Spasticity and hypertonia are problems you should be aware of, and you should most likely get this issue addressed in conjunction with your rehabilitation team. By not addressing spasticity and dystonia, you risk your muscles continuing to tighten up, further restricting your ease of movement and leading you toward the maladaptive spiral and a poorer quality of life.

- **Dehydration and fluid management** can also be a problem after stroke. Simple dehydration is one of the leading causes of emergency room care and rehospitalization within the first month. In the hospital, your doctors will monitor you closely for dehydration. However, after you go home, you will want to give special attention to your hydration status. Again, the onset of dehydration is insidious—patients do not necessarily know why they are feeling worse and worse as the days go on and their urine gets darker and more concentrated, as they get closer to kidney failure. Fortunately, the problem can usually be easily reversed with oral and/or intravenous fluids. But the long-term answer to this problem is quite simple—drink more fluids, and also monitor the color of your urine to ensure it is not getting too concentrated.

- **Spastic bladder** can become a problem over time. One reason most stroke patients avoid drinking adequate fluids is the difficulty they have getting to the toilet. Additionally, over time and insidiously, their bladders may actually develop some spasticity which leads to a problem called urge incontinence, meaning when they first feel the urge to urinate, they have to go immediately, or else incontinence occurs. Urge incontinence is a source of embarrassment, leading to lack of social engagement and a poorer quality of life. Medications from your doctor can really help the symptoms of urge incontinence; however, you must first know about the problem in order to work with your doctor on the solution.

- **Depression** is also sometimes a late complication with an insidious onset. Depression has been addressed in other chapters; however, it is important to recognize and monitor the "temperature of the water," by paying attention to your mood and your emotions. It's also important to avoid shame, which you may, unfortunately, be apt to feel. Seek help from family, friends, and your doctor. You have nothing to be ashamed of. Effective treatment is usually quite straightforward and can include medication, counseling, exercise, and support groups, among other things. Depression is also a factor that can lead toward the maladaptive spiral and a poorer quality of life.

- **Walking ability and walking speed** become important markers for your mobility. Basic mobility is necessary for you to be active in the community and engage with family and friends. Maintaining a good walking speed has many components, such as strength, endurance, spasticity, and pain control; these are complex issues that should be worked on with your rehabilitation physician and the rehabilitation team. However, one easy and objective way to measure progress or decline is the simple Ten-Meter Walk Test, in which your walking speed is measured over a set ten-meter course. Walking speed is highly correlated with an adaptive spiral and a higher quality of life.

Again, perhaps we all are like the frog swimming in the pot of water. Awareness of the factors that can lead to water of dangerously high temperatures is important in each of our lives to avoid unnecessary discomfort and difficulty.

Summary

The early complications after a stroke, as well as the later ones, can be managed, but everyone, including patients, families, and care teams, must be aware and vigilant to spot these complications. Otherwise, they might sneak up on us or be so insidious in their onset as not to be noticed. Avoiding complications equates to avoiding unnecessary struggles and can help keep you on the adaptive spiral for a better quality of life.

CHAPTER 15

ADAPTIVE SPIRAL AND THE PLASTIC BRAIN

Plasticity, then, in the wide sense of the word, means the possession of a structure weak enough to yield to an influence, but strong enough to not yield all at once. Organic matter, especially nervous tissue, seems endowed with a very extraordinary degree of plasticity.

— William James

The adaptive spiral is built on the foundation that, with intentional effort, we can change. For this to be the case, our brain must be able to change. And, specifically, an individual's psychological mindset must lead the way in order for long-term recovery from stroke to occur. That does not mean if you merely think positive thoughts, recovery will happen spontaneously. No amount of sedentary positive thinking will produce results if those thoughts are not translated into action. Stroke recovery equates to *active struggle and slow rising*. Motivated people will take action to change their brains. The psychology of change—active struggle through structured therapy—may be the determining factor for long-term success in stroke recovery. Therefore, rehabilitative activities ideally should start as soon as possible—when the patient is medically stable enough and able to participate. Functional recovery is defined as improvement in mobility and activities of daily living; it has long been known that it is influenced by structured rehabilitation.

Many processes happen in your brain after a stroke. They are generally grouped in terms of what happens early and what happens late.

Spontaneous Recovery

In the aftermath of stroke, your immediate purpose should be to do all you can for neurologic recovery. With your stroke, even early on, your brain is trying to preserve critical elements and functions for your body to be able to operate, even though your body may never function exactly the same again. In most cases, the brain will begin to set up for the process of healing right away. However, it's important to clarify that the process of healing is usually a process of "improvement over time," and not a complete resolution of symptoms.

Although this healing is imperceptible, your brain is very active in trying to heal and preserve as much brain capacity as possible. During the early days and weeks, the brain works to reduce the swelling (or edema) caused by the stroke's injury to brain tissue. Also, surrounding the core of the stroke damage (the cells in the core usually die quickly) are cells that become "stunned" or lose their capacity for normal function. These cells are not behaving normally, but they will return to healthy tissue again if the cells are nourished properly and stimulated by intentional activity. This region of cells around the core is called the penumbra. This surrounding area does have the capacity for returning to proper function. This process, in part, happens spontaneously, but the process can be aided by medical teams; for example, by restoration of optimal blood flow to the region. How to preserve these stunned cells is an area of intense research. Additionally, as the brain is intricately interconnected, a stroke injury to one part of the brain may set off a cascade of effects, which may temporarily produce widespread symptoms. The brain will, at least partially, recover function of these regions outside of the true stroke damage (sometimes called resolution of *diaschisis*). Each of these processes begins with stroke onset and occurs during the first 4-6 weeks after the stroke.

Neurological Reorganization

This 4-6 week window is by no means the end of the recovery period after stroke. A process called neurological reorganization in the brain plays an important role in the restoration of function. Neurological reorganization is a combination of spontaneous recovery and relearning through rehabilitation. It can extend for a much longer period of time than the resolution of brain swelling or restoration of blood flow to the penumbra.

Neurological reorganization is of particular interest because it can be influenced by rehabilitation training. This recovery-inducing reorganization requires cells to communicate and cooperate with each other. When the brain changes because of this reorganization, it's called neuroplasticity. Dr. Donald Hebb identified a fundamental concept in brain recovery when he stated, "When two neurons (nerve cells) in proximity (close together) fire together, their synaptic (cell-to-cell firing) connection is strengthened."[1] In other words, *cells that fire together, wire together.*

Rewiring portions of the brain, so to speak, requires patients to perform goal-directed behavior. The skill has to be meaningful for the patient—something the individual patient actually *wants* to relearn and that comes from numerous cells within the brain activity in a coordinated manner. Evidence shows that skill acquisition (ability to achieve a goal with consistency) drives neuroplastic changes in the brain, which means the behavior or activity needs to be truly important to the individual. This is called the saliency factor. This begs the question, "Whose goal is it anyway?" The patient's, the therapist's, or no one's at all? Rote, repetitive movement alone, won't measure up to the saliency factor. Therapeutic practice for stroke recovery should be functional and meaningful.

Specialty-trained therapists help and guide stroke patients through tasks that gently push the brain to improve and, over time, tasks become easier and easier. Thus, stroke recovery becomes a *relearning* process, facilitated through rehabilitation practice. Recent evidence suggests that this skill acquisition can take place months, years, and even decades after stroke, though slowly, if that individual is motivated enough to put in the hard work of practicing various goal-oriented tasks. Obviously, this reorganization process is heavily influenced by rehabilitation.

I experienced these concepts in rehabilitation training in my arm and my leg. However, it has always been easier, quicker, and less frustrating to reach over and do the task with my good arm. I have one normal side and one impaired and hemiplegic side, making it difficult for me to do simple, everyday tasks like turning a door handle or picking up a cereal box in my impaired hand. I am confident, however, that with consistent practice, I still have the potential for progress.

Conversely, I only have one mouth to generate speech. I can't resort to a "good side" to speak out of a "good mouth." In my case, the stroke caused a speech pattern called apraxia of speech. Apraxia is a neurologic disorder of movement planning and execution. Speech generation required an incredibly complex sequence of movement by lips, tongue, vocal cords, facial muscle, and even the diaphragm. These movements need to be coordinated with precision. For the first entire month after my stroke, I could barely figure out how to stick out my tongue, or voice simple one-syllable sounds. But I had no choice but to use my mouth for speech, for communication—to connect with the world.

I practiced the basic sounds intensely. Talking became a form of practice, which was very meaningful, and task specific. My speech improved…but over years. I've made all of the basic sounds in my vocabulary literally millions of times. My speech, however, still is not perfect, even after seventeen years.

To me, as a specialist in stroke rehabilitation, my speech improvement testifies to a few things. First, it highlights the concept of forced practice, in this case, for speaking. I was highly motivated to perform the task of speaking; in fact, I was forced to speak, even though it was extremely uncomfortable to do so. I felt high motivation, to the extent of forcing myself to keep trying and to extend the effort, day in and day out, because speaking is really an essential aspect of life for communication and maintaining and developing relationships. Moreover, I was highly motivated to perform this task with an increasingly high degree of precision, or suffer embarrassment every time I spoke. Indeed, embarrassment and shame is a barrier almost all stroke patients confront and are challenged to overcome. Brené Brown, a social psychologist and author, says shame is "an intense painful feeling or experience of believing that we are flawed and therefore unworthy of love and belonging—something we've experienced, done, or failed to do makes us unworthy of connection." She adds, "I don't believe shame is helpful or productive. In fact, I think shame is much more likely to be the source of destructive, hurtful behavior than the solution or cure."[2] The ability to overcome embarrassment and shame may actually be the determining factor in success, for if you have an adaptive spiral mindset, shame lessens, even to the point of extinction.

Finally, my speech improvement demonstrates that incremental changes over time with intense work are possible, but the results are usually not perfect restoration of how you were before the stroke. Nevertheless, it is worthwhile to make the effort for recovery. You will be in a pattern of upward adaptive spiral.

Facilitating Adaptive Spirals: The Power of Task-Specific, Repetitive, Goal-Oriented Practice

I've found that the same principles applied in regaining my speaking abilities as applied to regaining my walking abilities. In my extensive rehabilitation process, the desire to stand up and walk became a major driving force. Indeed, we are all highly motivated creatures when it comes to standing and walking. We see this innate drive in infants, and also in adults who have suffered from strokes or other orthopedic or neurological injuries. It is normal for people to take this ability for granted; only when it is taken away do we notice this yearning for strength to move as we please. Walking is natural, and I was highly motivated to perform this task, even though it was very uncomfortable. It was also necessary for me to perform it with an increasingly high degree of precision, or suffer embarrassment every time someone saw me walking and limping around. Having an adaptive spiral mindset was again important. The intentional and repetitive nature of these tasks is also important. I felt such motivation, to the extent of forcing myself to try, day in and day out, because walking is such an essential part of living in this world, of getting around, and of accessing the community, while playing a large role in an individual's ability to maintain and develop relationships.

In my medical practice, my colleagues and I are really facilitating neuroplasticity through the task-specific repetition of walking. We try to foster and support this walking behavior by first guiding the individual to walk independently, often with physical assistance from 1-3 people, or a harness hooked to a track on the ceiling. We sometime use a treadmill, with or without the harness. Once the patient is able to walk independently, with or without an assistive device, we start measuring the individual's walking speed. We do this with a short, ten-meter measured walk task in the clinic, and begin tracking the improvement to clinic visit to visit, which can be highly motivating to patients as they see real evidence of their improvement.

Walking speed does seem to matter a great deal. Patients able to force themselves to progressively walk faster are able to induce *speed-dependent adaptations* (body and limb muscle activation patterns) thought to improve the overall walking pattern after stroke.

We encourage walking behavior in a couple of ways. When I was younger, I was taught an important concept, which holds true with the walking behavior pattern: When we have a goal and measure it, we see additional improvement; when we report our accomplishment to others, the rate of improvement increases. Thus, we encourage patients to get a step-counter and track the number of steps taken over time. A usual step goal for someone early on in the recovery process is 1,000 steps per day, then 2,000, then 3,000. By this means, we are able to set goals, and the patient feels a real sense of accomplishment when they achieve them. We are also investigating novel social-media platforms to report the accomplishment of steps and distance traveled to a group of like-minded stroke survivors who are trying to accomplish the same step and distance goal.

Walking promotes a number of health-inducing factors, such as supporting an everyday activity, improving blood pressure control, improving aerobic conditioning, and better regulating fat and glucose stores. Again, it is worthwhile to make the effort for recovery. You may find satisfaction in overcoming the struggle, and may even find enjoyment in the journey. You will be in a pattern of adaptive spiral.

Rehabilitation and recovery of hand function after stroke, however, is more challenging in most cases. One reason is that humans can do most tasks with one hand. Using the impaired hand is usually quite frustrating, especially when a task is easily done with the non-impaired hand. Hand function is different from speech and walking behavior because of the good hand always being ready to perform the task. Often, *learned non-use* is a barrier people have to overcome. Learned non-use is a behavior pattern of learning so many methods to accommodate for a hand impairment that the impaired hand falls into disuse, even while the hand has some unused potential.

Thus, it's often necessary to discourage use of the good arm and hand to foster use of the impaired hand and arm. We often prescribe a program that does just that so the patient remembers to try, and try again, and persists with the impaired arm. This program is called constraint-induced movement therapy, as mentioned in Chapter 4 when I talked about spending sixteen days participating in a research study in

Alabama a few months after my stroke. The concept is just as its name implies: Constraining the good hand with a mitt (which makes use of the good hand more difficult) to force use of the impaired hand. This forced use can be very frustrating, and brain change happens only over long periods of time. Furthermore, the brain change is imperceptible to the person changing, so we time the various tasks we ask patients to practice and perform. Timing the tasks creates immediate feedback and is highly motivating. Patients want badly to beat their previous time to prove they are improving. And they usually do improve, but it takes a long time...and their improvement may be less than complete and less than expected. I know this because of my time spent doing constraint-induced movement therapy. Thankfully, I did improve, but the improvement was less than I had expected. I had come nearly to the end of my neurologic restoration; I felt I had to move on to other recovery efforts and activities toward the adaptation side of the recovery coin.

One simple measure I recommend to patients to facilitate constraint-induced movement therapy principles is almost too simple to be taken seriously. In my clinic, I see dozens of patients who have some ability, though limited, to extend their fingers on their impaired hand. I ask these patients to do a simple task: for one or two hours a day, wear an oven mitt on their good hand, thereby constraining their strong hand and reminding them to use, and invariably struggle with, their impaired hand. And, invariably, out of the dozens of patients I have urged to do this, not one, to my knowledge, has ever tried this technique. Perhaps the psychological pressure to do things with the easy hand is just too great. I get it—I certainly do.

Nevertheless, for those of us who have achieved even a little improvement in hand and arm function, it is a very worthwhile effort. You may find nuggets of joy in the struggle, and you may find enjoyment in the journey. While working and struggling, you will be in a pattern of adaptive spiral.

The Two Sides of the Function Coin

As mentioned in Chapter 13, for most people, neurological restoration will only take you so far; restorative efforts do not bring the stroke survivor back to 100 percent. It is important not to neglect the "function" coin—adaptation to impairments. We can effectively compensate... despite the impairments that may remain. In this sense, for most survivors of stroke, both sides of the coin are critical to long-term success. The way you navigate these two sides of the same coin will largely determine your successful return to life and function in your home and community.

Your stroke is not like a mechanical problem to be "fixed." For example, with a car, the mechanic would tell you what is needed to get the car back in working order. You would agree, and the mechanic would get the work done. Recovery from a stroke is not like that. Recovery takes individual effort, usually guided by a team. You can find joy in the struggle, the struggle of life. And adaptation and compensation can take place, leading to relearning of the activities you enjoy. Your hardship may be more extreme than others who have not had a stroke, but my hope is that every one of us can develop this adaptive spiral pattern and find enjoyment in the journey by focusing on both sides of the function coin.

Optimally, you will surround yourself with people who have a growth ideology for your new life to take root. With this mindset, we can all be like gardeners—patients, family members, doctors, therapists, and nurses alike. The gardener plants a sapling, carefully turns the soil, making sure the new growth gets the right nutrients and the right balance of sun and shade. The gardener trusts the plant to grow as healthily as possible. As you seek assistance from rehabilitation specialists who will attempt to nurture you back to full health, it is your responsibility (as the tree in this analogy) to do the hard work of growth—to struggle to reach for the nourishing light and to manage the nourishing water—so that elements inside of you (from neurological sprouting to growth in character) may slowly rise to become a vibrant tree again, and even bear fruit to provide nourishment to others. In this way, you can continue with life's purpose and create a meaningful life.

Summary

Although the brain is a very complex organ, it can change if properly stimulated. Initially, change happens fairly quickly; later brain changes take focused effort and a highly motivated individual. However, the formula for change and improvement is task-specific, repetitive, and goal-oriented practice. Over time, although almost indiscernible to the individual, those who engage in this concept will slowly rise.

CHAPTER 16

SPASTICITY AND THE FREEDOM TO MOVE

I move, therefore I am.

— Haruki Murakami

Of all the late complications of stroke with their respective adverse effects on individuals, spasticity can have the greatest chronic, long-term effect on movement. Spasticity and hypertonia are defined, in simple terms, as an increase in muscle tone (on the spectrum of flaccid to rigid), especially when the joint and muscle is moved rapidly. Spasticity is felt as excessive tightness on the already-impaired side of the body. Spasticity magnifies the weakness and the functional impairments caused by stroke. Hypertonia may also be defined as increased muscle tone at rest.

Unfortunately, for many reasons, spasticity usually gets minimal attention from healthcare providers. Furthermore, the timing and onset of spasticity are insidious enough that it evades the attention of the care providers and the patients themselves, who are wondering why it's getting harder to move and walk, day after day. They often think it must be something they are doing, or maybe something they are neglecting to do. It doesn't help that the typical onset of spasticity and hypertonia is at 2-3 months, precisely the timeframe of typical therapy programs to taper off. This makes many stroke patients feel guilty and even ashamed that they aren't able to maintain the hard-fought gains they achieved while they participated in skilled therapy. Thus, poorly informed about the process, timing, and treatment options for spasticity and hypertonia, they often start down the maladaptive spiral of inactivity; if you can't move well, it often leads to a pattern of poor mood, unhealthy eating, and obesity.

Additionally, it is often truly difficult to find good and comprehensive spasticity management healthcare services. In fact, in the Mountain West region, we operate the only comprehensive spasticity management clinic within a 500-mile radius at the University of Utah. This is the main reason I perform clinical care for hundreds of patients with spasticity and have done numerous studies on different treatment methods for spasticity. It is so hard for many patients to get comprehensive spasticity and hypertonia treatments that they fly into Salt Lake every few months just to come to our spasticity management clinic.

Spasticity and hypertonia make muscles especially difficult to move voluntarily or through range-of-motion stretching exercises. Either or both conditions can develop after stroke. About 38 percent of patients who are initially hospitalized but later discharge to a home environment develop one or both of these conditions.[1] The effects of spasticity and hypertonia create muscle tightness, which can be uncomfortable, make movement such as walking or using your arm difficult, and lead to stiff and contracted joints. A wide range of spasticity and hypertonia severity exists in patients, from the mildest cases to the severe, bound up by their own muscles.

Spasticity management is a clear and unmet need for many stroke patients; thus, I have a passion to deliver care and education and to further research efforts on spasticity and hypertonia. However, spasticity management is not going to cure all of a patient's ills. Take the impaired fingers and wrist, for example. Most patients with spasticity have three main deficits in their arm: lack of strength, impaired sensations, and spastic muscles. Spasticity management treatments don't return strength or sensation. However, if one muscle group is tight, spastic, and binding up the muscle, loosening that muscle can produce more functional movement because the patient can now flex and extend more easily. This loosening effect can make a profound and significant difference on the ability to move the muscle.

Stroke patients often hold the hypertonic arm with tight, spastic fingers that form a fist. It can be very painful for a patient to move out of this position, and it limits the affected limb's functional use.

Consider another example of a patient with severe leg and trunk spasticity and hypertonia. A patient's comfortable walking speed directly relates to their ability to access the community. The ease at which individuals can move freely around their environment and the community bears great significance on quality of life. Freeing spastic muscles by loosening them essentially frees the individual to do more activities they enjoy. The person is then freer to engage in activities that foster the adaptive spiral.

As a clinician, one of the most unfortunate circumstances I see in a patient, one who has successfully recovered the ability to walk independently after weeks in inpatient rehabilitation care, is to have spasticity subtly and insidiously take away their ability to walk. The muscles slowly tighten and bind up the patient, making walking slow, difficult, and energy-consuming. By the time the patient reaches me, often the spasticity has caused their knees and ankles to become contracted, which usually requires orthopedic surgery to correct.

Assessment of Spasticity

The doctor treating spasticity and hypertonia should focus on objective measurements of tone and evaluate the functional impairments caused by the spasticity. For example, the doctor will check range of motion and sensation, and also observe your walking pattern because spasticity may increase with activity (as opposed to being at rest). The

Modified Ashworth Scale is often used specifically to measure spasticity in the limbs.

Spasticity clinics will have excellent communication between all clinicians and their patients, related to goals the patients want to achieve. Clinicians know that functional goals, such as improvements in ease of dressing, functional use of the hand, gait quality, walking stability, and walking speed are significant for patients.

Collaborative Victory

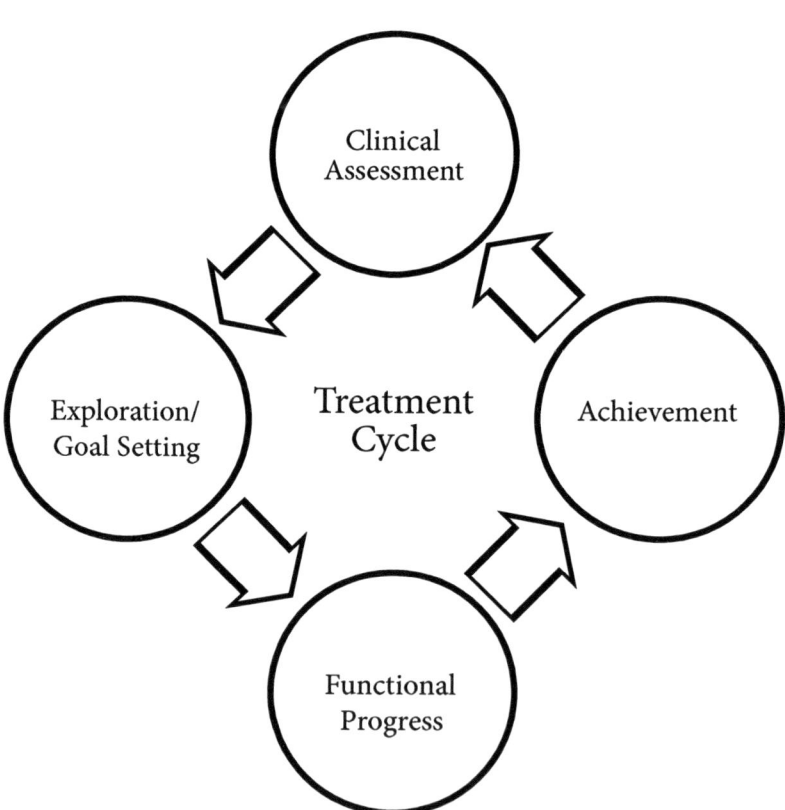

However, to obtain the gains from any spasticity management strategy, patients must exert focused and directed effort into therapeutic activities. Your doctor may talk to you about appropriate goal setting. In my clinic, we use the treatment cycle mentioned previously, which is an excellent tool to apply to overcome the barrier of spasticity.

The cycles usually take place in a three-month interval. Each cycle should include:

- Clinical assessment focused on spasticity, including clinical tests, assessments of walking, walking speed, etc.)
- Appropriate goal setting, i.e., exploring what matters to the patient.
- Functional progress achieved by performance of therapeutic activities, usually with the support of therapists.
- Achievement of goals. Then, if necessary, the process starts over with reassessments.

Following this process, you and your doctor will be able to communicate, engage, and work together for what matters most to you. This pattern will facilitate the type of therapy that will give the greatest chances for your success in spasticity management.

Treatment for Spasticity

The good news is numerous treatment options are available for the management of spasticity and hypertonia. All of the treatment options should be focused on reducing spasticity and hypertonia-related symptoms, thereby improving quality of life by optimizing functional use of the limbs and preventing limb contractures (locked joints). Management of spasticity and hypertonia should be centered on optimizing functional use of the limbs and preventing contractures.

Spasticity management clinics may employ use of oral medications, botulinum neurotoxin injections (Botox is currently the most common option), phenol (alcohol) injections, and baclofen pump management, along with physical and occupational therapy, stretching, and surgical procedures. Your doctor will recommend specific treatments, which should all be used in combination to achieve specific, directed functional and therapeutic goals.

Also, daily stretching, especially of the shoulder, wrist, fingers, hip, and ankles is critical for the prevention of contractures. The use of static or dynamic splints may also be helpful.

Oral Medications

Oral medications are often useful when the treatment of muscle spasticity and hypertonia involves several areas or if spasticity-related pain is present. Most medications alter the function of nerves, but these medications do not pose a serious risk of irreversible side effects. The four FDA-approved oral medications to treat spasticity in adults include baclofen, diazepam, dantrolene sodium, and tizanidine.

All the commonly used oral medications can have side effects, mostly mild drowsiness, but sometimes these medications affect cognition and alertness and cause alterations in mood. Patients can potentially adjust to these untoward side effects over time, but they are something for you to be aware of. All in all, oral antispasticity medications have been shown to be somewhat helpful; unfortunately, oral medications alone have not been shown to consistently improve active function in stroke patients. However, when used within a broader treatment strategy, they can help achieve excellent results.

Botulinum Toxin Injections

Botulinum toxin can be thought of as a potent muscle relaxant that only acts locally on the muscle injected. Botulinum toxin injections are fairly easy to perform, have a repeatable effect, and have few side effects. Injection of botulinum toxin can improve the use of spastic limbs and enable improvements in activities of daily living, decrease complications such as skin breakdown and contractures, and lessen the burden on caregivers. However, it is sometimes difficult to find doctors with spasticity management experience using botulinum toxin injections. Doctors who perform botulinum toxin injections generally have extensive knowledge about muscle surface anatomy, muscle activation patterns, and spastic muscles' effect on function, and they usually treat a lot of patients with spasticity, such as at a major medical center.

Phenol (Alcohol) Injections

Phenol, a form of alcohol, has a therapeutic effect when injected around nerves and has been used successfully for many decades for spasticity management. Your doctor may suggest this option when spasticity is localized to just a few areas, but the spasticity in those locations is severe. Your doctor may use muscle stimulation using a needle for optimal localization of the phenol injection. Phenol injections have the advantage of rapid onset of action; they increase the effect's duration compared to botulinum toxin injection, and they are much more cost-effective. However, painful nerve-type sensations may emerge, depending on the nerves injected. Be sure to inquire about these injections' possible complications and side effects.

Intrathecal Baclofen Pump

Your doctor may suggest intrathecal baclofen, delivered by an implantable infusion pump, which has been effectively used to decrease moderate to severe spasticity and hypertonia, especially in cases where the hypertonia is widespread, affecting many muscles in several muscle regions. Because intrathecal baclofen therapy is more precisely localized at the specific site that modulates spasticity within the nervous system, it uses a small fraction of baclofen, with better results, than any oral baclofen medication. Thus, intrathecal baclofen may be better tolerated without unwanted effects when compared with oral anti-spasticity medications. Intrathecal baclofen therapy, in combination with physical therapy, may also improve walking speed and overall walking ability in patients with spastic hemiplegia after stroke. Furthermore, intrathecal baclofen therapy has been shown to improve quality of life, reduce spastic hypertonia, and improve overall function.

Unfortunately, overdose or withdrawal from intrathecal baclofen therapy can cause serious and sometimes fatal effects, due to malfunction in the pump or disruption in the pump catheter. Education and information about these risks and benefits should be carefully considered and weighed in consultation with your doctor.

Surgical Management

Surgical measures aimed at the brain, spinal cord, peripheral nerves, or muscles are sometimes used for the goal of improving spasticity and hypertonia. Your spasticity management physician will be able to explore all of these options with you.

Often, the use of oral medications, botulinum toxin, phenol injections, intrathecal baclofen therapy, stretching modalities, and surgical release are used in combination to achieve specific, directed functional and therapeutic goals. Also, therapeutic strategies should be individualized to patients' needs by therapists who are familiar with treatment of hypertonia because no two patients are exactly alike.

My Personal Experience with Spasticity

I have had mild spasticity, which I have treated effectively with oral medications and occasional botulinum toxin injections. A few years after my stroke, I was able to wean off the oral medications and stop the occasional botulinum toxin. I had my own spasticity pretty much under control. Then, fifteen years later, I had a terrible cycling accident, with multiple injuries and a significant concussion. As opposed to the substantial recovery of my stroke fifteen years earlier, my cycling accident produced injuries that were mainly orthopedic—broken ribs, contusions, separated shoulder—but the thing that affected me for the longest time and became the most significant barrier to my function was the increase in the spasticity that I thought was in the distant past. This return of spasticity, in a sense, was the most surprising aspect of my recovery. However, this cycling injury offered me the opportunity to experience spasticity in isolation. I wasn't working on a whole host of other deficits as I was at the time of my stroke. I was just fighting against the actually mild barrier to my freedom to move. That slight restriction of my freedom to move was surprisingly psychologically taxing and even affected my confidence. I dealt with the spasticity with several months of oral medications and a few rounds of Botox. As my soft-tissue injuries and bones healed over many months, the pliability in my legs returned and the spasticity lessened. Nevertheless, this experience made me realize more completely what my spasticity patients deal with, including their emotional and psychological fight to stave off the maladaptive spiral and press forward to their full potential. A slight degree of spasticity stays with me, and probably always will, which serves as a subtle reminder of the need to always push forward in spite of external and internal forces that would hold stroke survivors back.

Summary

Spasticity management is clearly an unmet need for many stroke patients. There is a need to deliver care, perform education, and further the research efforts on spasticity and hypertonia. Fortunately, numerous treatment options exist for the management of spasticity and hypertonia. If you have spasticity and hypertonia, the use of oral medications, botulinum toxin injections, phenol injection, the use of the baclofen pump, and surgical managements should be explored. Close collaboration with a spasticity management team is ideal. Treatment for spasticity and hypertonia may aid in your attempts to foster and nurture an adaptive spiral leading to higher quality of life.

CHAPTER 17

STROKE IN THE YOUNG: UNIQUE ISSUES OF DRIVING, WORKING, AND OTHER ASPECTS

Just as we develop our physical muscles through overcoming opposition—such as lifting weights—we develop our character muscles by overcoming challenges and adversity.

— Stephen R. Covey

Although more likely in older people, stroke can occur at any age. When stroke happens to the young, it affects their lives, families, social roles, and careers in different ways than the older population. In the young stroke population, the patient may be the main income-earner for the family, with most of life ahead of them, which can make a stroke especially devastating.

About 33 percent of stroke patients are less than sixty-five years of age. Stroke, therefore, interrupts the working population. Moreover, approximately 10 percent of stroke patients are less than fifty years old. Of the 800,000 new strokes in the United States each year, that's 80,000 relatively young people. These patients have a long life expectancy during a demanding time of life in which they are beginning their families and building their careers. Young stroke survivors make up a special population with unique demands and needs.

Rehabilitation strategies for elderly patients are not always applicable for younger patients. Thus, in the context of young peoples' unique life circumstances, it's often challenging to meet their needs in the traditional rehabilitation setting geared toward the elderly. While stroke can affect physical and cognitive skills at any age, younger stroke survivors are at a life stage when employment is important. Additionally, they are more likely to be caring for children. Their recreational hobbies and interests are different, their social interests are different, etc. Consequently, young stroke patients' needs are not being addressed as robustly at many inpatient rehabilitation centers, which can affect a young person's quality of life for the next several decades.

As a stroke rehabilitation specialist and a young stroke survivor myself, I feel for many of these young stroke patients who only have limited life experiences to lean on rather than the emotional reserves older patients have built up. Their lives have just come crashing down—critical elements of their being, of who they are, have been stripped from them, including speech, strength, sensation, coordination, cognition, and even the ability to swallow. Getting these young stroke patients back on their feet and assuming roles in their families and communities is of paramount importance.

Risk factors are also different in the young stroke population. For all age groups, the most common risk factors are smoking, hypertension (high blood pressure), high cholesterol, alcohol abuse, race (more common in patients of African descent), and migraines (more common in female patients). Hypertension seems to play a bigger role among younger stroke patients, with hypertension leading to bleeding or aneurysm and arteriovenous malformation (AVM) rupture (leading to hemorrhagic stroke) being more common in the young. There is also an unusually high risk of death in the first twenty years after stroke—about 27 percent.[1]

Younger patients are more likely to return to the home environment, which is a very positive thing for most patients. However, even young stroke survivors with seemingly excellent outcomes are often found to have worse potential for anxiety and depression. Additionally, likely due to young stroke patients' increased life demands and stressors, a lack of attention may be paid to their cognitive impairments and how they affect their disability. These cognitive impairments can complicate a young stroke patient's reintegration back into the community and return to work.

When this special population is studied, these young stroke patients value exercise and fitness programs, education programs, individual counseling, stress management programs, and recreation and social programs. Adaptation of young stroke patients in the home and work environment, and in social functioning, is commonly addressed. It is especially important to set these people, who have decades of life still to live, on the path of the adaptive spiral and on to a high quality of life.

Driving

Driving is an important issue to many stroke patients as they reintegrate into their previous roles. To many people, driving after stroke represents quality of life, autonomy, fulfillment of life roles, access to leisure pursuits, and engagement in other meaningful activities. This is especially true for the young stroke survivor, who desires to be independent in such things as employment and driving, and wants to develop advanced life skills for many years to come. However, driving an automobile is a complicated multi-task activity. Safe driving performance requires successful integration of sensory, strength, coordination, and cognitive functions, including perception, decision making, information processing, and attention. You and your team of rehabilitation specialists should have the common goal of getting you out on the road, while ensuring safety.

All told, partially because the typical stroke patient is in their seventies or eighties, only about 30 percent of stroke survivors ever return to driving a car. Still, out of the people who return to driving, almost

90 percent do not receive any formal evaluation of driving ability.[2] This poses special problems for returning to driving, with its inherent risks to self and others, because some stroke patients have a poor ability to recognize their own cognitive and/or physical limitations. They may have neglect syndrome where one side of their attention is not perceived, or they may have medical conditions besides the stroke such as seizure disorders, diabetes mellitus, and cardiac disease, which can affect driving performance. Indeed, as much as driving is an important life skill, it is also fraught with risk and danger.

Multiple ways to attempt to predict driving safety after stroke have been identified, the most reliable being by a multidisciplinary team consisting of a physician and specially trained therapists. That means, ideally, your doctor would review your readiness to be referred to a specially-trained group of therapists who would do a thorough evaluation. When the physician feels confident about the patient's cognitive, visual, and motor abilities, these specialists will do additional screening tests and also assess reaction time and tests of road knowledge. Assessment concerning the practical application of driving skills, such as gas, brake, and steering coordination, and residential and freeway driving abilities may be conducted. However, the most reliable way to predict success in driving is a formal on-the-road driving assessment that evaluates the physical, motor, visual, and cognitive elements essential for safe driving. Therapists should also make recommendations on specific equipment and strategies to make the stroke patient a safer driver. These adaptations include items such as blind spot mirrors, spinner knobs, left-foot accelerators, pedal guards, turn-signal extensions and hand controls. Virtual driver simulation programs, done in the safety of a clinic setting, are another important tool in the formal driver evaluation.

Unfortunately, patients with aphasia who demonstrate safe-driving ability may fail in their efforts to renew their driver's license because of difficulty with the written exams. In these cases, the physician can advise the licensing authority to make reasonable accommodations for the patient's language deficits.

In most cases, the physician will complete a Functional Abilities form, based on the recommendations of the specialized therapy evaluation. This will be submitted to the respective state's Division of Motor Vehicles office. Once again, you and your team of rehabilitation specialists should have the common goal of getting you out on the road, but ensuring safety for you, your passengers, and the other people on the road.

Return to Work

It is important that you have a personal internal conversation about realistic goals and wishes for your life. This internal conversation is important so you will know your limits, but also your potential. There are indeed limits, which may be very personal and complex. Whatever you decide, it should still be a decision. If you are near retirement age, you have a choice: return to work or seek volunteer options, travel opportunities, or a whole host of other activities. However, it is imperative that you do something—that you make your choice.

Research on stroke patients' outcomes indicates that most stroke patients do not get back to the vocational or professional responsibilities they once had. Adaptation is usually required; the ability to make changes and be flexible is paramount. However, even stroke patients who have retired from full-time work should endeavor to return to their previous post-retirement activities or find new activities. Meaningful engagement with the community will significantly affect quality of life.

Although no predictive model for return to work after stroke has been established, an interesting picture is emerging through recent studies. Half of the patients who complete a comprehensive inpatient rehabilitation program geared toward pre-vocational and vocational activities are able to return to work, if they so choose. Of that half, 50 percent return to work only part-time after the stroke; furthermore, about 60 percent of the people who successfully return to work (full-time or part-time) require some modification because of changes in their abilities.[3] Again, the ability to adapt and be flexible is key.

Several factors make successful return to work more likely, including being age fifty-five or younger, holding a prior professional or managerial position, having a higher education level, and having a prior moderately high-income level.[4]

Alternately, barriers for reemployment have been linked to severity of stroke, which is intuitive—the more impaired a person is, the less likely they will successfully return to work. The presence of aphasia also creates a significant barrier to return to work. Additional return-to-work factors include existence of other health and physical challenges, prior job satisfaction, job characteristics, personality, social support, and mood disorders.

In my experience, patients who desire to return to work should be encouraged to maintain contact with employers in the early post-stroke period. This lets the employer know the patient will be working toward a goal of returning to work.

Recommendations often include a gradual return to work in a supervised setting with appropriate accommodations based on impairments, safety concerns, and/or the potential for overwhelming psychological stress. It is also often helpful to think of return-to-work efforts based on four different strategies, depending on the patient's stroke characteristics. Each strategy will be distinct based on the individual and include difficulties and impairments with speech/language, cognition, mood, and physical abilities.

1. **Speech and Language (Expressive Aphasia)**

    A person's speech and language ability is among the most profound losses one can experience. Even slight trouble with finding the right word from time to time can significantly affect a person's confidence to the degree that many patients lack the self-assurance to attempt reentry into the work environment. Speech and language difficulties are barriers people have to wrestle with every day.

It helps to realize that everyone, your coworker included, have some challenges of their own. Your speech difficulties after stroke are more obvious to you and your coworkers. But these deficits are not insurmountable; the difference between you and those around you is merely a matter of degree and not a matter of being the only one who has problems. As much as possible, it helps to decide before each and every day that there is nothing that anyone can say or do to make you feel ashamed of your speech.

In my experience, two individuals come to mind who have very successfully reentered the workplace with expressive aphasia. Both are in their forties, with a couple of decades of work still to be achieved. Both are professionals—one is an attorney and the other an architect. Both have strong support groups, including family, friends, and coworkers. But there is something about each of them, something intangible and hard to measure. This intangible asset is best described as self-confidence—the need to believe in oneself. I have the utmost respect for the trial attorney who has the self-confidence to muster up the courage to go to battle on a case in front of a judge and twelve members of the jury. He does this as he wrestles with his speech, speaking publicly on a grand stage. He does what it takes to be successful.

2. **Cognitive Deficits (Relating to Logical Thought, Awareness, and Mental Processes)**

Cognition deficits come in multiple forms and various degrees of severity. Taking the cognitive deficits from Wernicke's aphasia and dementia out of the picture (which are generally more severe and long-standing), most of the cognitive deficits after stroke share a few common things. People with cognitive deficits from stroke often have problems with judgment, lack insight into their deficits, and are frequently impulsive. As such, strategies to facilitate return to work should be done through collaboration with an interdisciplinary team and with a firm understanding of stroke's long-term consequences. These deficits are complex to manage when trying to get people back to work. People with cognitive deficit are often a little overconfident, making it a struggle for them to make the best decisions.

I typically employ a few strategies when working with stroke patients who have cognitive deficits and want to return to work. First, I urge the patient to be cautious and not take things too fast. Second, I encourage them to seek advice from trusted counselors, including family, friends, coworkers, and even their employer. Lastly, it is especially important to take a neuropsychological test from a specialist to assess cognitive strengths and weaknesses. This test is basically a long, in-depth assessment of the patient's reasoning, memory, ability to make good judgments, ability to divide their attention (pay attention to more than one thing without getting distracted), etc. Based on the test results, the interdisciplinary team can create successful strategies to overcome any barriers.

When returning to work, it is especially important to do so in stages. Also, it's important to find a trusted coworker to have dialogue with about your performance on an ongoing basis, and also have some designated supervision for a period of time.

Sometimes a patient surprises me by going from a low level of cognitive function right after stroke to returning to the highest levels of professional life. Such was the case when a young college president arrived by life-flight to the University Hospital. He had left-sided weakness and neurological neglect syndrome—a right middle cerebral artery stroke. In the early days after his stroke, his brain began to swell, which necessitated the neurosurgeon to remove a large portion of his skull to relieve the pressure building up in his brain. I knew that, based on the location of his stroke, cognitive function might be a major problem. Initially quite drowsy, he eventually became alert enough to participate and be guided through the recovery process. He recovered some strength, and then a little more, and in time, he was up on his feet, and then walking. It took a long time and a lot of work by him, and all of us, but his recovery exceeded all of our expectations in terms of strength and cognition.

He had the goal of returning to his former position as college president, which was especially challenging because of his level of responsibility. We prepared him for the multitude of activities he would be called upon to perform. The outpatient speech therapist did role-playing activities, having him practice conducting meetings, interacting with colleagues, and practicing public speaking, along with his regular strengthening and coordination therapy. Eventually, the college's Board of Trustees provided supervision and feedback in his unique workplace. Once back at work, he navigated the workplace environment, making adaptations as necessary. It thrilled me fourteen months after his stroke when he sent me a DVD of his speech, in full cap and gown, at the college commencement exercises.

Other examples don't go so smoothly. More recently, a young junior high teacher returned to work, also with a neurologic neglect syndrome. While dealing with some misbehaving eighth graders, he got frustrated, lost his temper, and sent one boy to a dark broom closet. In hindsight, he knew it wasn't the right thing to do, and the principal and school district had to put him on probation while they worked with him. Luckily, his school principal was understanding and beneficent, so he is now off his probationary status and doing very well.

Unfortunately, it is always difficult to predict who will recover adequately from a cognition standpoint. It's usually a game of return to work, then supervise from multiple perspectives, encourage adaptation, and monitor.

3. **Mood**

    Depression and anxiety are more common if you have had a stroke. Even with mild depression, you may lack full motivation to seek employment and push yourself physically, cognitively, and emotionally. It is important to give yourself ample time to heal both your body and mind. Your physician should be a resource in these situations, and will provide appropriate medications and referral to a counselor.

    Sometimes patients feel just a little overwhelmed about jumping back into life when they don't feel normal, or as normal as they once were. At times, this can be called an adjustment disorder, which basically means trouble adjusting to the patient's "new normal." Patients often feel filled with regret, uncertainty, and a lack of self-confidence. Referral to a rehabilitation psychologist can be very helpful, so they can talk through various issues, come up with strategies, and build up confidence levels. Remember, things do not have to return to the same as before your stroke for you to return to a high quality of life. It's important to explore the possibilities of your new life and make necessary adaptations.

4. **Physical impairments**

    Your rehabilitation team will address physical requirements specific to your workplace. When you are deemed ready for reemployment, you are encouraged to work closely with your employer for any accommodations you may need. The physician should provide education materials for the employer, as well as recommendations for return-to-work activities. The use of adaptive equipment and technologies should be explored since those measures can further enhance functional capacity in the workplace.

The Americans with Disabilities Act provides protection of rights of disabled citizens, and employers are responsible for providing reasonable accommodations to disabled workers. Employers are also prohibited from making hiring decisions based on a disability if the potential worker is able to perform the job's key components.

Some people won't be able to return to their prior occupations. This is an unfortunate effect of some strokes. If you want to return to work, which is generally recommended if you are able, you should seek guidance from a vocational counselor provided by the state or community. If you are motivated to do so, consider enrollment in a vocational rehabilitation program that provides job retraining and reeducation, as well as counseling.

Summary

Young stroke survivors often face challenges unique to the young population, specifically because of their stage of life, higher demands and expectations on them, and a greater life expectancy. Whether a patient can return to work is dependent on many factors, but stroke patients should be allowed and encouraged to maximize their functional outcome potential in the community, including, when appropriate, resumption of employment.

There is hope after stroke, but usually things will not go back to the way they were. You may have to adapt to a new situation; you may even have to reinvent yourself. But the power is within you to do that reinvention and regain a high quality of life.

The recreational aspects important to many stroke survivors, but especially to the young, are addressed in Chapter 20.

CHAPTER 18

STAGES OF LIFE AND LOSS, AND THE POTENTIAL TO REPURPOSE LOSS FOR GOOD

"Without a bit of sadness, a beautiful samba cannot be made."

— Vinicius de Morais and Baden Powell

Grieving the Loss of Function

Ann was an active and independent seventy-eight-year-old woman. A widow of five years, she never slowed down in life's parade of activities; she was involved with her bridge club and took an active role with her grandkids and great-grandkids. The years kept slipping away. That all changed when one morning she woke up and couldn't move her right leg. Her leg felt normal to the touch, but her strength was just gone—the leg was paralyzed. She reached for her phone, realizing her speech was slurred when she called her daughter.

When I met Ann, she was just two days into what she called "her strange, bizarre ordeal." The stroke was caused by a pea-sized clot that had formed in her heart because of atrial fibrillation. The clot had lodged itself in the front part of the left brain in the anterior cerebral artery. What she thought was a strange and bizarre ordeal was really a very common occurrence, but no less terrifying to her.

A stroke in the anterior cerebral artery territory produces paralysis of the opposite side, and the leg is more affected than the arm. Independent walking continues to be a struggle for these patients, even long-term. However, most of the time, the affected arm and hand returns to full or nearly full function.

At day two, Ann's speech had almost returned to normal, and her right arm and hand were just slightly weak and uncoordinated, but she had little to no strength in her right leg. Over the next days, weeks, and months of therapy, walking and leg strength were to evade her.

Standing up and walking represents and is more complex than just putting two feet underneath you and working your body upright—it signifies one's independence and one's sense of self-worth. When something as rudimentary as standing and walking is lost, in most cases it represents a major psychological blow. Sometimes physical function and psychological feeling of loss become intertwined. Too often, it's very difficult to unwind and unravel the tightly-wound mess. To lose the ability to do something so basic, so fundamental as walking, is no small thing.

The Uses of Worry

Worry and anxiety of loss or even death are natural components of what it means to be alive and conscious. Indeed, the conscious awareness of our mortal limitations are a part of life—that we grow old, that many things that happen to our bodies are beyond our control, that living things die…and it's okay. That knowledge can even become a beautiful part of life; while life's seasons give way to losses, we accumulate intangible elements like wisdom and experience.

It is important to realize we have different seasons of life, and in each season, we value things differently. Social psychologist Erik Erikson proposed a useful model with separate and distinct stages of life and tasks that we work toward and value. When stroke afflicts someone, the person may feel a heightened sense of loss of self-worth related to the current stage of life. Understanding this sense of loss can help the stroke survivor's family and support community to give more effective support. People very close to the stroke survivor may be going through their own sense of loss. Knowledge of these stages after stroke can focus attention and recovery efforts on the things most valued by the stroke survivor, and the people closest to them.

In early adulthood (20-39 years of age), we tend to value "love," and the desire for intimacy over isolation dominates our value system. After stroke, an overarching question exists: "Can I love?" or rather, "Can I *still* love?" I often think of the twenty-two-year-old father of an infant boy who seemed to have based his whole recovery effort on being able to be a good dad. Years have passed, and the love between that young father and his little boy is tangible to all who encounter them. Stroke survivors, in most cases, are capable of forming intimate, reciprocal relationships (e.g., through close friendships, partnerships, or marriage) and willingly make the sacrifices and compromises that such relationships require. If a stroke survivor is unable to form these intimate relationships, even for a time, a sense of isolation may result, arousing feelings of darkness and angst. We can facilitate these relationship skills through support groups, community involvement, adaptive recreational groups, and showing love and support for stroke survivors. A primary goal is allowing the stroke survivor to gain confidence in social situations.[1]

In middle adulthood (40-59 years of age), we tend to value care and desire to have an active, meaningful life rather than a stagnant one (something Erikson called *generativity*). The overarching question becomes "Can I make my life count?" or rather, "Can I *still* make my life count?" During middle age, the primary developmental task is one of contributing to society and helping to guide future generations. When a person makes a contribution during this period, perhaps by raising a family or working toward the betterment of society, a sense of productivity and accomplishment results. In contrast, someone unable to help society move forward, because of a stroke or other physical or mental difficulty, may develop a feeling of stagnation—a dissatisfaction with their relative lack of productivity. We can encourage and provide resources for stroke survivors. Vocational rehabilitation programs, job retraining programs, and even volunteer opportunities are to be encouraged, with the goal of community reintegration.[2]

In late adulthood (60 years and older), we tend to value *wisdom* and desire a sense of our own meaning and importance rather than giving into despair over what our lives have been (something Erikson called *ego integrity*). The overarching question then becomes, "Is it okay to have been me?" or rather "Is it *still* okay to have been me?" As we grow older and become senior citizens, we tend to slow down our productivity and explore life as a retired person. During this time, we contemplate our accomplishments and seek clarity on whether we have been leading a successful life. If stroke occurs during this stage, individuals may see their lives as unproductive, or see themselves as a burden to society, thereby becoming dissatisfied with life and developing *despair*, which often leads to depression and hopelessness. A primary goal is to help stroke survivors by reminding them of their impact for good in their family that lives on, and in encouraging them to be active in doing what they can to carry on the good aspects of their legacy.

Though stroke and stroke-related disability cause major turmoil at any stage of life, it's through understanding the things we value that we can take steps to alter the course, to lead to adaptation and acceptance of our lives. Our task is to take painful loss at the stage we are in—and the anxieties that such loss brings—and amalgamize it into greater understanding, peace, and even joy.[3]

The Way We Deal With Grief

The way we deal with grief is critically important, for it can propel us to further growth in an adaptive spiral, or cause us to wallow in despair.

In her 1969 book *On Death and Dying*, Dr. Elisabeth Kübler-Ross, an international expert on grief and grieving, introduced a model now widely used. She admits, "Grief is the shattering of many conscious and unconscious beliefs about what our lives are supposed to look like. Those are our beliefs, our hopes, our fantasies, the way life should unfold."[4] Sooner or later, people find ways to cope and move on, but they usually do so in a predictable pattern.

The Kübler-Ross model is popularly known as the five stages of grief, though more accurately, the model postulates a progression of emotional states experienced by people suffering from a loss. Although Kübler-Ross's model primarily looks at death and bereavement, it's a helpful model for loss in general, including the profound and severe loss of function after stroke. In 1995, Kübler-Ross, herself, suffered a series of strokes that caused loss of some functionality; perhaps her prior work on grieving helped her cope with the losses she incurred. Whatever the case, she was able to carry on to further achievement with her work in psychology until her death in 2004.

The five stages of death and dying that Kübler-Ross identified, as they relate to stroke, are:

Denial: In this stage, individuals believe the diagnosis is somehow mistaken, and cling to a false reality—a reality that they prefer. In the case of stroke and loss of function, it's hard to deny your experience, as most stroke victims suffer the worst losses right away. However, there can be some denial about the long-term consequence, expecting a 100 percent recovery, which is not the norm. Nevertheless, it is critical to have a realistic hope of recovering an acceptable quality of life.

Anger: When the individual recognizes the extent of loss from stroke, they may become frustrated. A typical psychological response during this phase would be:

Why me? It's not fair! How can this happen to me? Who is to blame? Why would this happen?

Usually, no one is to blame for a stroke, and it is important eventually to move on to a future-focused outlook.

Bargaining: The third stage involves the hope that the individual can strike a deal for restoration of the previous lifestyle in exchange for a reformed lifestyle. It is quite natural for individuals to try to strike a deal with a Higher Power of their choosing since some people believe a stroke is an effort by God to get the patient back on the right track. If you are inclined to this pattern of thought, again, it's important to see God as the champion of your recovery, not the afflicter of punishment.

Depression: This stage involves depression of mood, thinking, *I'm so sad; why bother with anything? Things are never going to be the same, so what's the point?*

Blame and guilt can be used, like everything else, to distract ourselves from the pain of loss.… Often there are no answers to the question of why it happened. The survivors have to be spared this question in order to live. The individual despairs at the recognition of their mortality. In this state, the individual may become silent, refuse visitors, and spend much of the time mournful and sullen.

Acceptance: The final stage is acceptance of what has occurred and a knowledge that "It's going to be okay." In this last stage, individuals embrace their inevitable future, work to change what is within their control, and learn to accept what is out of their control.

Often, these five stages go on as inner, subconscious dialogues. Looking back years later, I realize that I, too, went through these stages, and on to acceptance. The five stages are part of the framework that makes up our learning to live with what we have lost. Kübler-Ross said that "the truth is that life is risky and dangerous and we are the only species on earth who knows that and as much as we fear it, [loss and] death will come to each of us one day."⁵

The twelfth century poem, "'Tis a Fearful Thing," by Yehuda HaLevi resonates with me, perhaps because it represents to me tender feelings about profound loss and even death.

> 'Tis a fearful thing
> to love what death [and loss] can touch.
>
> A fearful thing
> to love, to hope, to dream, to be—
>
> to be,
> And oh, to lose.
>
> A thing for fools, this,
>
> And a holy thing,
>
> a holy thing
> to love....
>
> To remember this brings painful joy.
>
> 'Tis a human thing, love,
>
> a holy thing, to love
> what death [and loss] has touched.

Being Your Authentic Self

According to Brené Brown, the original definition of *courage* is to tell the story of who you are with your whole heart. She touts the courage to be imperfect and the compassion to be kind to ourselves first, and then to others. When we are our imperfect, authentic self, we embrace the belief that "what makes us vulnerable…also makes us beautiful."[6] Exhibiting the courage to be vulnerable makes us more likely to succeed at recovery, and in life, whatever our challenges might be. And, in life, what we find success in ultimately makes us happier.

True happiness is something everyone desires. However, it's often a mistake to pursue materialism and status as the way to true happiness. From both a religious and scientific context, happiness and sorrow exist so that we can appreciate and comprehend the magnitude of the blessings we normally enjoy. Dr. Richard Davidson, founder of the Center for Healthy Minds, describes happiness as "the capacity to remain upbeat and to sustain positive emotion over time," and he explains that there is no such thing as pleasure without pain.[7] Often, true richness and happiness in life come from first experiencing profound loss.

When a person goes through a trial, the depths of a person's agony may actually enable that person, at other times, to appreciate joy and happiness. The human mind and brain is surprisingly resilient. Humans not only overcome difficult events quickly, but they generally rise above the difficulty and come out of adversity as happier people.[8]

Science and health writer Henry Dreher explains, "Research has shown that our health is protected when we express a full range of emotions, including the so-called negative ones. When we find constructive ways to express anger, grief and fear, we prevent lapses into hopelessness, depression and passivity.… Unless we explore and express these primary human emotions, we cannot receive the information they carry."[9]

Your loss of physical function due to a stroke can provide an opportunity for great growth of character, which may offset that painful loss. Overcoming trials and the new perspective learned after any significant challenge can bring a sense of accomplishment and joy, leading to strength and fortitude.

Furthermore, we can and do make changes in our brain on a daily basis, including in our capacity to appreciate and experience happiness. Davidson says, "We can take most responsibility for our own brains, and shape our brains wittingly in a more intentional way by cultivating healthy habits of the mind."[10]

One way to gain true and lasting happiness stems from our ability to build loving relationships. Also, participation and engagement in an active community help us internalize and obtain true joy and happiness. Happiness is built on the foundation of deeper emotions like an appreciation of the life you have, on the positive connections you have built with others, and on the achievements that give you a sense of personal pride.

We are "wired" to respond to the simplest of things so we may be happy. Humans are generally moral and good, and we have evidence of this in both a religious and scientific context. Davidson explains, "There are a number of…strong empirical findings which are consistent in showing that we indeed come into the world with this quality of innate basic goodness. What we're doing is nurturing seeds which are already present."[11] But that goodness can also be learned and strengthened.

It's easy to judge yourself when your subconscious mind delivers unattractive and unappealing messages about you and your purpose within your family, workplace, or society. Too often, people feel like they are not measuring up to a certain standard and engage in persistent self-criticisms. Embrace vulnerability. Be a little easier on yourself and on others. Take more deep breaths in your labors and interactions. Realize that no one is perfect, and we also can't expect perfection in ourselves. We can focus on the journey and on the process of improvement. Recognizing improvement in our performance and behaviors is one way to gain happiness.

Research shows that the capacity to foster relationships leads to long-term happiness.[12] Love is likely happiness in its truest form and is a very powerful motivating factor. Love between husband and wife. Love between father and daughter, mother and son. Perhaps this love is what Helen Keller meant by fidelity to a higher purpose—that purpose of loving one another. Love is the balm that says, "Your best effort is good enough," "I accept you in your vulnerability," and "I am here for you in your time of grieving your loss."

Summary

We will all suffer loss at one time or another—being broken and having to pick up the pieces of our lives is part of the human condition. Loss will mean different things at different points in our lives and development. In many situations, we can repurpose the loss we have experienced, accept it, and in some cases, recognize the good that has come out of it. Being able to see the small victories in a seeming defeat is one key to being resilient, leading to a high quality of life.

CHAPTER 19

RESILIENCE

Strong people alone know how to organize their suffering so as to bear only the most necessary pain.

— Emil Dorian, *The Quality of Witness*

Despite all of life's trials and tribulations, we can and do overcome most of the distractions and struggles of the natural world we live in. "Resilience is the virtue that enables people to move through hardship and become better," says former Navy SEAL and author Eric Greitens. "No one escapes pain, fear, and suffering. Yet from pain can come wisdom, from fear can come courage, from suffering can come strength—if we have the virtue of resilience."[1] But we have to choose to live a resilient life.

Fight On

Because of my personal experience with stroke, I have the unique opportunity to develop relationships with patients who are going through the hardest trial of their lives. Because I share the same type of experience with pain, fear, and suffering, I can connect with these patients in a way other physicians may not be able to.

Life can still be pretty great, no matter our situation, and perhaps that is in part due to facing and overcoming challenges. Our struggles take on new meaning when our struggles meet *purpose*.

I recently followed up with a patient, a friend, really, whom I had been seeing for the last seven years. Claire lives near Jackson, Wyoming. She had a stroke in the prime of her life at age forty-three. It happened on a Tuesday in late spring as she was running on a trail beside the Snake River where it runs below the foothills of the majestic Teton mountain range near her home. She had been trying to run each day, up and down mountain canyon trails with names like "Paintbrush Canyon" and "Cascade Canyon," but running beside the Snake River was her normal route on Tuesdays. She had an idyllic life: married, two kids, and living in an Edenic place. As she was running, she noticed a bald eagle circling high above. One can only imagine the scene, in all its splendor and glory, and the way she must have felt, soaking it in through all her five senses, which were processed by her brain, as she had done so many times before.

Then, without notice, her brain failed to function the way she was used to. She began to feel weak in her left leg, then stumbled, and again stumbled, this time falling to the ground. The type of stroke she was having not only made one-half of her body weak, or even paralyzed, but also affected the cognition function, making her confused about what was going on and the appropriate next steps in this crisis situation. She was more confused and distracted than alarmed by the situation as she lay on her back, looking up at the eagle overhead.

Eventually, a pair of fishermen on a drift boat on the river spotted her lying on the trail. When they approached, she was confused and calmly asked them to call her husband to pick her up. The fishermen, clearly sensing something was seriously wrong, called 911 and initiated medical attention. Claire had been thrust from what she considered an ideal life to the harsh world of hospitals, treatments, medicine, and doctors, in a multi-year effort to regain an element of her previous quality of life.

She is now fifty-three. Every three months, Claire makes the flight from Jackson to the University of Utah Medical Center in Salt Lake City for treatments and procedures for spasticity—treatments she can't find in her hometown. Over the years, we have become friends; my daughter and her son were born just weeks apart. She loves to travel with her husband and family, and I love hearing about her new adventures. I've always been somewhat surprised that she has remained fairly impaired in her mobility. She is always glad to see me, in spite of the painful series of injections I give her spastic muscles. And I, of course, am always glad to see her even though I give her spastic muscles a quite painful series of injections.

The last time Claire visited me was after six months (she had missed her regular three-month appointment), and she told me that three months earlier she had fallen on the ice in Jackson and ruptured her spleen. The spleen had to be removed and she required a few units of blood, and something unexpected appeared on the routine imaging: a tumor in her abdomen. The tumor, which was subsequently removed, was found to be a cancerous sarcoma. She is now on an adventure of a different sort—trying to survive a potentially deadly cancer. We both cried in my exam room, lamenting the problems that so commonly beset our human bodies. I mourned for her; she has been through so much, and, through adaptations, had reached an acceptable quality of life. She says now her goal is to see her grandchildren born, to hold them in her arms, but I ached for the uncertainty this new diagnosis brought. The world we live in can be so cruel. But Claire fights on, determined to make the most of her life, however long she has left, with purpose and joy.

Disappointments and tragedies occur in all our lives. It's a sad and sobering fact. But those disappointments don't have to remain bitter moments. They can become treasured experiences we see as sweet and that help us learn.

A Glass Half-Full

Factors exist in all of our lives that can transform bitter things into sweet ones. Given a half-full glass, we can always look at the full half portion and be grateful for what we have, rather than fixate on the half-empty side. We all have many disappointing experiences. We could all dwell on the negative if we so choose. However, we have the power to turn that thinking around by recognizing the things we can do and being grateful for what we have. Gratitude is an often-overlooked virtue. A correlation exists between gratitude and happiness. Happy people adapt to challenges and find happiness in the changes.

Although I am by no means a perfect role model, I can bike, ski, and hike. These are things I *can* do, individually or with others, that give me hope. The ability to continue to enjoy the outdoors is truly one of my greatest blessings.

We can also look at the half-empty portion, ask what can be done about it, and then go to work to change the situation. The power is within us to have that attitude and make that choice, based on our own self-confidence and motivation, the first platform of the adaptive spiral. For stroke survivors, this is the essence of the two-sided, precious "recovery" coin—neurological restoration and adaptive compensation.

It is easy to have the mindset that the world owes us sweetness and happiness, but that is not how things are in our natural world, where we grow by hard experiences. In fact, many of life's experiences are like walking through an overgrown rose garden. When we are in the thick of the garden, sometimes all we feel are thorn scratches and scrapes, but looking from a little distance, all we can see is beauty. But, oh, the glorious scent of the roses!

Happiness is a state of mind, heavily influenced by our expectations: what we think about what the world gives us and what we think about how life should behave. If nothing can be done about difficult situations, as is often the case, it is crucial to *control our response* through believing in ourselves, choosing to channel our regrets, and finding fulfillment in other activities. These other activities may end up being more fulfilling than the original course you were on, partly because of the sense of fulfillment that comes from realizing you can overcome a challenge. We can make peace with difficult situations, even when life does not work out according to our preconceived ideas. In very simple terms, we are happy if life meets our expectations. The challenge we all face is adjusting, or adapting, our expectations. That is my definition of resilience.

Post-Traumatic Growth

One area of observation and research in the last couple of decades has been exploration of what makes people resilient and brings them happiness, including after a stroke. There is some evidence that our brains may, in fact, be "hard-wired" for resiliency and to respond and yearn for the things that bring fulfillment and happiness. Surprisingly, there is now a wide and growing recognition that people may actually report some positive psychological changes following a traumatic event such as a stroke in addition to the common negative emotions. The term "post-traumatic growth" has been applied to these perceived positive changes, previously called an *adaptive spiral*.[2] I'll mention a few key features of resiliency here.

Resiliency depends, in large part, on one's ability to secure healthy roles in family and community relationships. Usually, adaptations must be made after a stroke or brain injury, including possible major shuffling of roles and responsibilities. Now that you have to revise your role in the family and community, you can set goals you couldn't have while in your former roles. Reaching for and accomplishing these goals can improve your relationships. Again, adaptations will be necessary, but sometimes, relationships are improved after serious neurological injury.[3]

Studies show that coping with loss optimally involves not only "getting over it and moving on," but also creating meaning to facilitate the best recovery.[4] Families and strong support systems can create the meaning by "providing a way to craft narratives about the changes that have occurred, and by offering perspectives that can be integrated into schema change."5 The words we use and the stories we tell about our situation deeply affect how we think about it.

For example, Sue, a young patient in her early-fifties, had a stroke after a car accident. The trauma to her neck ended up tearing a small flap in the inner lining of her carotid artery (this is called arterial dissection), and clotting factors in her blood eventually collected at the arterial tear site and broke off, traveling to the brain and causing a stroke. Sue suffered speech impairments and numbness and weakness of her right side. Sue's husband advocated and supported her in her challenges. The couple learned about the joys of adaptive recreation, and both of them became heavily involved in a charitable organization that helps people be more active in the outdoors. Each time I see them, they show me videos of them skiing and traveling. Sue's husband, with his engineering background, designed and created a side-by-side recumbent bicycle that they can both enjoy together. As a couple, they have developed the mantra that, because of Sue's stroke, she has discovered her "superhero strength," which is simply knowing what is important in life. The stroke, in their family narrative, was the key to unlocking this door of discovery. Today, Sue frequently speaks to groups and her enthusiasm is contagious.

A Harvard study has followed the lives of scores of people over the age of seventy-five pertaining to the ability to achieve and maintain happiness. Dr. Robert Waldinder, the current lead researcher of the study team, says a main conclusion has been that "good relationships keep us happier and healthier."6 Apparently, our brains are wired to yearn to build relationships with others. Deep, long-lasting friendships aid in socialization and are important both psychologically and physiologically.

However, after a stroke, physical mobility problems often hamper the ability to socialize; a good rehabilitation team will problem-solve to overcome this barrier. For example, they may create support groups and recreational groups of individuals with similar interests. Whether we are physically impaired or fully mobile, adaptations are always necessary in all our lives.

Additionally, a growing body of evidence suggests that physical activity and exercise support resiliency.[7] We can literally transform our brain through intentional effort, and one of the best ways is through physical activity, specifically aerobic exercise. It is especially helpful when we engage in novel and varied physical activities. This positive effect increases when the activities are done outdoors. That our world is so beautiful and our human brains respond and are receptive to this beauty is a rich blessing. Input from all our senses—sight, sound, smell, touch, and taste—sends a flood of pleasure that can create a virtual symphony in our minds.

It is challenging to behave in accordance with these few factors, but when we do, we are taking steps toward more resiliency; we can nourish our brain to obtain additional happiness in our lives.

Our lives are full of challenges, both large and small. By developing resiliency, we can face severe challenges and attain happiness and a high quality of life.

What We Choose to See Determines Our Character

I am often surprised by patients' resiliency of spirit and their will to live and progress. For example, C. J. was a twenty-two-year-old construction worker when he fell twenty feet off a landing. Amazingly, he popped right up and said, "Get back to work. I'm fine," but he collapsed to the ground a few moments later. Both sides of his arteries that fed a region of the brainstem called the pons had burst, and he suffered a catastrophic stroke. Ambulances came and intubated him to begin mechanical ventilation (using a machine to breathe for him). He quickly went from the ER to the ICU. When the doctors assessed him, they saw no signs of brain activity based on the absence of spontaneous movement. However, C. J. remembers the doctors telling his mother, "We ought to just turn the machines off; his brain is already dead." Luckily, his mother insisted on checking to make sure. Sure enough, his *mind* was still functioning adequately. Through the weeks and months that ensued, C. J. had some spontaneous recovery and was eventually able to wean himself off mechanical ventilation. His swallow returned so he could eat some foods and he was weaned off his feeding tube. He began to have some movement of his mouth, enough to voice one-word requests. He was also able to control a computer mouse with assistive technology devices, enough to write complex thoughts and expressions. He used his intact intelligence to enroll in college and complete courses.

In my clinic today, looking into C. J.'s intelligent eyes, broken body aside, I feel as though I'm peering into his soul to see a profile of courage. I asked him one probing question: "Out of all the painful and trying experiences of the last nineteen years, are you still glad to be alive?" He replied, in his labored and breathy voice, with an enthusiastic "Definitely!" I perceived that if he were physically able, he would have shouted for joy in that moment. I have to wonder if, over the nineteen years, he has made the adaptations needed to do the critical things for happiness: count his blessings, thrive in a redefined social and familial role setting, learn novel ways to socialize, and gain from the sensory experience of the outdoors. If someone like C. J., despite losing so much, can count each day as a blessing, those of us not so severely afflicted can take courage from his example.

Summary

As humans, we all have wounds—physical, emotional, and sometimes neurological. Sometimes those wounds are profound. But we have uncommon strength when we realize our resilient spirits and nature, especially when we can find purpose. Ernest Hemingway said, "The world breaks every one, and afterward, many are strong at the broken places."[8] Even being broken…perhaps *because* of being broken, light can seep into our lives and we can be strong.

CHAPTER 20

NATURE'S RESTORATIVE POWER

But are not exercise and the open air within the reach of us all?

— Walt Whitman

In her book *The Nature Fix: Why Nature Makes Us Happier, Healthier, and More Creative*, Florence Williams tries to uncover the science behind nature's positive effects on the brain.

Williams explains Attention Restoration Theory, which states that when a person is outside in nature, they are "drawn into this state of soft fascination in which our attentional networks get a little bit of a break. We start experiencing the world through our senses." Our nervous system quiets down a little and we can recharge rather than be merely running around dousing fires. In other words, we can "take time to smell the roses." When we're in this more comfortable state, our mood increases and we just feel better.

Another well-known social science theory, the Stress-Reduction Theory, suggests the nervous system response drives the emotion of happiness, while nature exposure simply and immediately lowers our anxiety and stress levels. Reduced anxiety and stress essentially lower the background noise in our lives; we can think more clearly and mood improves.[1]

In an interview with *Camping Magazine*, Williams stated:

> I concluded that maybe it's not the pathway that matters, but that our brains evolved in nature and there is some very fundamental comfort that kicks in. We were made to take in oxygen from the trees. On some level our bodies and brains just relax when we're outside. As long as we know that being outside facilitates other health effects—fresh air, exercise, being connected with our friends, being disconnected from technology—there are all these amazing things that come together when we're outside.[2]

Spending prolonged periods of time in nature, such as hiking or camping—exploring our natural world, the second platform on the adaptive spiral—helps us survey new possibilities and make sense of life when the world feels upside-down. Having time to ponder some of the big questions is critically important. We have time for questions about who we are in the world and what the stroke changes about who we are… our lives and our dreams. Often, the experience of stress, grief, or trauma in the aftermath of stroke can make extended periods of time outside therapeutic and healing.

The Power of Nature to Heal the Mind

For me, just being able to access the outdoors after my stroke was initially questionable. Being outdoors now brings a measure of independence; often you don't value a thing until it's taken away for a time. Fortunately, my physical recovery has allowed me still to do many meaningful outdoor activities. It took a lot of work to regain the ability to participate in some of my former recreational activities, but I knew the value of those activities and that they would add to my life satisfaction. One benefit to living in Utah is amazing access to outdoor recreational opportunities. We have mountains to ski, hike, and bike, wonderful national parks, desert canyons to explore, and lakes and rivers to discover.

For centuries, writers like Thoreau and Whitman have advised us to spend more time in nature. They feel a tension between the urban world's technology and our need for the simplicity of the natural, wild world.

The technology we are all bombarded with, and the drive to multitask, places unnatural demands on our brain's pre-frontal cortex, which is involved with critical thinking, impulse control, problem solving, decision making, and strategic planning. This situation is further amplified by stroke because some of those brain systems are already taxed—sometimes to capacity—causing unwanted and excessive fatigue.

To be fair, technology has always been with us, beginning with our early ancestors who mastered fire. "Technology is always a double-edged sword," says David Strayer, a professor in Cognitive and Neural Science at the University of Utah. Take, for example, the cell phone. "More recently, smart phones allow us to be connected with technology anytime we want. In essence, we are spending more and more time interacting with a device and less and less time interacting with people or exploring the natural world."[3]

But nature is a restorative tool. Studies measuring brain activity of people even just walking in a tree-filled park show a resting effect from their usual state of multi-tasking. And to get the full restorative benefits, you need to leave the technology behind, "thereby engulfing yourself with the mind-quieting effects of nature," says David Strayer. Sherry Turkle, a researcher at the Massachusetts Institute of Technology adds, "Our capacities for empathy and self-reflection do appear to be challenged—even atrophying—as our digital interactions replace analog ones. One happy solution…spending more time in unwired places. One of the underappreciated benefits of venturing into [the outdoors] is that we are often thrown into connecting with each other."[4]

Physical Activity's Role in Healing

I love skiing. Although I am not as good as I was before my stroke, I love the cool, crisp mountain air, and with each turn on my skis, I get a little rush. Using only one ski pole to accommodate for my stroke-weakened right side, with my right ski acting more like a rudder on a boat, my strong left side and my two strong hips do the work of carving turns and navigating me down the mountain. Sailing on two skis—not too fast to be out of control—through the natural beauty of the mountains and forests in the winter, I feel free and unencumbered by life's trivial concerns.

While I love to ski with a companion, I also love the solitary skiing experience as I work to turn and glide down the mountain. For me, skiing is a valued, even treasured, activity; for a time, it looked like regaining a level of freedom so I could ski was an impossibility—a pipe dream. The desire, work, and effort I expended made getting on the mountain again after my stroke and the fulfillment of my goal a more meaningful achievement. Just as Henry David Thoreau went to the woods nearly two centuries ago, I go to the mountains "to live deep and suck the marrow of life."[5] Being outdoors now brings a measure of independence, which was at one time taken away from me. Maybe it's not the highest form of happiness, but it puts my mind into the proper frame to appreciate and contemplate this life, and my loving relationships in it. It refreshes my spirit. It makes me thankful for the blessings in my life. It may not add years to my life, but it adds life to my years.

For healthy recreation, stroke survivors need to overcome barriers, including embarrassment and shame, physical challenges, and poor fitness levels. This combination often leads to few, if any, outdoor recreational opportunities and must be combated.

To accommodate for these challenges, at the University of Utah, we take advantage of the resources right in our backyard by creating an adaptive recreational program called TRAILS (Technology Recreation Access Independence Lifestyle Sports). Its mission and purpose is to promote community activities and outdoor recreational opportunities for people with neurological injuries, like stroke and spinal cord injury, as well as others with similar physical challenges. TRAILS aims to enhance the emotional and physical wellbeing of participants in a safe environment with a range of activities directed at a wide spectrum of functional levels.

People may report positive as well as negative psychological changes following a traumatic event, such as stroke, if they are enriched with nature and exercise. Thus, by using the synergistic effects of nature and exercise in this special population of stroke survivors, we are trying to nurture the mind and brain to promote healing. Within a few hundred meters of the Craig H. Neilsen Rehabilitation Hospital is the beautiful Red Butte Arboretum, giving patients ample opportunities to, at the very least, sample nature's restorative powers. Other research teams, including those at Stanford and elsewhere, have measured patients' moods, anxiety, and rumination levels, and found better memory and attention after walking in nature; the patients were also happier.[6]

Overcoming Physical and Emotional Barriers

"Everybody should have access to recreation. When a traumatic neurological injury occurs to a person, it's really important for the survivor to still have an outlet to engage with the outdoors," states Dr. Jeffrey Rosenbluth who, along with Tanja Kari, started the TRAILS adaptive recreation program to enable all people to enjoy the breadth of activities that Utah has to offer. Kari, a twelve-time medalist over four Paralympic games in cross-country skiing, says, "You can never have too much fitness outdoors. I have been fortunate to help hundreds of injured athletes learn to adapt and thrive in their chosen activity." Dr. Rosenbluth adds, "Daily participation in physical activity, including sport and recreation, is an important component of general health, and it is even more pertinent for individuals with neurological injuries."[7] When recreation and sport is a formalized component of rehabilitation, you will gain the knowledge and resources necessary to participate in a healthy lifestyle and avoid the maladaptive spiral with its secondary health complications.

Participation in recreational activities for people with a prior stroke is often restricted because of health concerns. These health concerns can be real, but they often are not as big a barrier nor as major a concern as many survivors think. Your physician can tell you what conditions to be cautious of, and if there are any physical restrictions. Armed with this knowledge, you can be more confident in the activities allowed so as not to self-limit, as many stroke patients do, based on their worries and misinformation. Recreation allows stroke patients to be more socially connected, plus positive attitudes pertaining to how you view yourself as an athlete correlate to your ability and vigor when participating in recreational activities.

In addition to attitudes, other barriers to accessing adaptive recreational opportunities include being unsure of a safe activity level, not self-identifying as an athlete, and the physical accessibility to the community. Addressing the barriers, physical and psychological, can be done with help from your rehabilitation team. For instance, many rehabilitation team members can teach you new adaptive recreation skills, equip you with the right equipment and resources, and encourage you. With the common occurrence of self-doubt, stroke survivors can often do more than they might think possible to achieve greater enjoyment out of life. Achieving competency in recreational activities can carry over to greater confidence and motivation in other aspects of life, thus facilitating the adaptive spiral. Ultimately, this leads to a higher quality of life, fewer secondary health conditions, and lower healthcare costs.

Jim, a twenty-four-year-old stroke survivor, is one inspiring example of success. His stroke left him paralyzed on the left half of his body at twenty-one, and he faced a steep climb of recovery. He went through the inpatient rehabilitation program for his stroke and began working on his impairment in the outpatient setting. He had been a high school hockey player just a few years before the stroke. He was eager, like so many stroke patients, to have a recreational and physical outlet to challenge himself, push himself, and compete—it didn't much matter if he was only competing with himself. When we introduced him to the adaptive recreation program at the University of Utah, he was all in. He started cycling one of our three-wheeled recumbent bikes. His bike was low to the ground, adequately stable, with clip-in shoes and pedals to provide extra support for his weak and uncoordinated left ankle and foot. Recumbent cycling became a great outlet for him, an activity where he could work up a sweat and have satisfaction. Recumbent cycles like this are quite expensive, but local grants offset their expense. Jim applied and was given a grant to purchase his own cycle. Now he cycles two or three times a week, and in the winter, he cycles around the indoor track encircling the Olympic speed skating oval in Salt Lake City. When asked about his experience, he says, "Having been knocked down by this stroke, it means a ton to me to be able to enjoy the outdoors, the community, and a new social riding group. When I'm on the cycle, working hard, it is one of the precious few times that I really feel normal again."[8] Perhaps "working hard and feeling normal" is something we all yearn for, whether we have had a stroke or are completely able-bodied. There is a power in supporting the physical exercise that leads to enhancement of the human spirit and the adaptive spiral.

Summary

The thrust to experience the world through our five senses in nature should not be taken away, especially not from the neurologically injured, who may need it most. However, unique physical and psychological barriers must be overcome. Through adaptive recreational programs, those barriers can be alleviated or eliminated, and confidence can be recovered. Nature truly has the ability to be a restorative tool.

When you are knocked down but get up again, when you encounter challenges but conquer them, your confidence soars and your stress levels plummet. Your productivity improves and you feel better. And to think, all this is available to you, just out your back door.

CHAPTER 21

CAREGIVERS OF STROKE PATIENTS: UNSUNG HEROES

No one is useless in this world who lightens the burdens of another.

— Charles Dickens

Stroke patients often require a period where they need assistance for basic or complex tasks, especially early in the recovery process. Sometimes, there is a period of partial or complete dependency, which may span months or even years. The people who deliver this care—spouses, partners, children, siblings, parents—are called caregivers. This chapter is for you, the kind, generous, and long-suffering caregiver.

Some hard and frankly terrible situations occasionally arise for caregivers. You may be giving care to a loved one with cognitive impairment, dementia, or profound physical limitations. You may be providing care for a disabled spouse with severe impairments and issues. If the marriage relationship was not perfect (and no marriage is perfect), pre-stroke marriage conflicts are often amplified. Psychological and emotional barriers to intimacy may arise for couples to work through. Antipathy or outright hostility between family members and the person now needing care and assistance sometimes develops.

Although caregiving is a daunting and sometimes thankless task, the service caregivers provide in the home is critical for many stroke patients to survive comfortably in their home environment. Success in this pursuit will be defined differently in almost every situation, but here are some key points to think about along your caregiving path.

Educate Yourself

Despite the shock of having your loved one changed by a stroke, either physically, cognitively, emotionally (or all three), it is important to be an active and engaged learner. Much of the information you will be given from the health professionals will be totally new—information about what causes stroke, the physical, cognitive, and emotional consequences, and the specific assistance your loved one will need. Everything will not completely sink in at first. Following are some of the key points to understand when you take on the caregiver role.

One of the biggest hurdles for caregivers is knowledge. Where I work, we encourage family members and caregivers to seek opportunities to ask questions about such things as the common early complications, late complications, and strategies to avoid these complications as much as possible. Also, be open to receiving training on practical caregiver requirements such as bracing, transferring, preventing mobility issues, and dealing with bowel and bladder issues. Chances are your rehabilitation center will have similar people dedicated to education of patients and family members. You should be provided with in-depth education about stroke, coping strategies for patients and caregivers, and coordinating efforts from other rehabilitation team members to teach you the skills specific to individual stroke syndromes and needs. Overall, assess your loved one's needs as well as your ability to meet them. The stroke survivor's healthcare team can help you determine what kind of help will be needed.

There can be a lot to learn, so take advantage of every opportunity to learn about stroke and your loved one's condition and prognosis. Be aware of the concept of adaptive spiral and maladaptive spiral. Be an active participant with the rehabilitation team in promoting and encouraging the patient to do more physical and cognitive activity—doing more leads to more neurologic recovery and higher emotional wellbeing and confidence.

Take part in support groups or programs offered by the hospital. It is extremely important to know you're not alone in your caregiver struggles. Talk with the healthcare team about what the stroke recovery and rehabilitation process will be. "Knowledge is power," says Pat Goodin, licensed social worker for the University of Utah Stroke Rehabilitation Program. "The more you know about stroke and specifically the stroke you are dealing with [in this case, the stroke of your loved one], the more empowered you will be to help your loved one move forward."[1] When you have a clear understanding of the stroke's location and its effects on the stroke survivor's ability to be at home and in the community, you will be better prepared to cope and make plans for continued care and gathering of resources and support options.

Attend a few therapy sessions so you can support your loved one during stroke recovery. Goodin advises, "By watching sessions, you can learn the skills needed to best help your loved one help him- or herself."[2] Pay attention to what the therapists do in each session and repeat those words and actions between sessions. For example, say things such as, "Hold your fork this way," "Here is your cup," and "May I hand you a washcloth?", instead of performing tasks for them. Even small accomplishments will help your loved one become more self-reliant and confident. By attending therapy sessions, you can also see progress and step in when it's time to learn skills needed to care for your loved one at home.

Prepare yourself financially. As Goodin says, "Gaining access to financial information is imperative early on."[3] Ask financial institutions what their guidelines are, and gain or execute power of attorney, if needed. Inquire about financial resources such as assistance with home modification, caregiving services, household help, meals, etc., so you can plan for future help and respite care. Get to know your insurance benefits and get access to your insurance case manager.

Caregivers will usually have to wade through the seemingly endless maze of insurance coverage. Medicare and/or health insurance will cover most of the hospitalization and rehabilitation expenses, but restrictions may exist on which facilities and providers are covered. So be sure to find out exactly what is covered and what out-of-pocket payments may be needed.

Range of Caregiving Needs

A caregiver may have sudden oversight responsibilities for multiple needs. Caregivers often need to:

1. Provide personal care such as bathing, dressing, and toileting.
2. Coordinate healthcare needs, including medications and doctor and rehabilitation appointments.
3. Manage finances and insurance coverage.
4. Help the survivor maintain and increase their ability to function and their quality of life.

Thinking about giving this type of care to a loved one is, for most people, a new experience, so they are sometimes overwhelmed. However, the tasks may become less overwhelming when the rehabilitation team guides caregivers through the process and demystifies it, breaking it down into practical, manageable steps.

Remember that you can't do everything. Try to be realistic with yourself about what you can take on and what you may need help with. Attending therapy sessions will help you set reasonable expectations of yourself, and help you determine when it would be best to hire professional help.

Coming Home

Once your loved one leaves the hospital, the situation's reality may begin to sink in for both of you. Here are things to consider as you take on your new roles.

Consider safety. You may notice stair climbing is extremely difficult; you may want to begin plans for an electric stairlift at home to improve accessibility. Ask the occupational therapist if you need to do anything to make the home safer. Often your occupational or physical therapist may suggest home evaluation of safety hazards before going home from the hospital or rehabilitation center. The therapists can make suggestions to help increase your chances of success at home and decrease risk of falls or other injuries. You may need to move the bedroom to another floor to avoid stairs, get rid of throw rugs to help prevent falls, or put grab bars and seats in the bathroom and shower.

Be aware of behavior and mood changes. Depending on the stroke location, behavior or mood changes may become evident. Many emotions can bubble up in relation to the "new normal." Refrain from using statements like "I know how you feel," Goodin recommends.[4] Instead use phrases like "tell me more about your feelings." The losses from stroke, whether temporary or permanent, can be devastating to the survivor. Active listening is more powerful than talking. Grief is a natural outcome after stroke. Be patient with the process as your life normalizes again. Feeling grief is a necessary step toward accepting life after stroke, for the caregiver as well as the patient.

Be on the lookout for depression. Stroke survivors are at risk for depression—30-50 percent are affected. Depression can interfere with your loved one's recovery. Ask the doctor what to look for and seek treatment right away if you see signs of depression, such as lack of interest in enjoyable activities, decreased appetite, or extreme moodiness. Psychologists and counselors are available in the outpatient setting for follow up if depression symptoms become obvious. Reach out to professionals for help.

Know the risk factors for a second stroke. Having a stroke puts survivors at a higher risk for a second stroke, so it's important to help minimize that risk. Prepare healthy meals with lots of fruits and vegetables, encourage exercise, make your home a smoke-free zone, and be sure your loved one takes medications as prescribed and keeps doctor appointments. Know the warning signs of stroke and seek help immediately if they arise.

Seek help from outside sources. Getting outside help can make all the difference in your ability to balance your life with your loved one's needs. Respite care can give you time apart so you can relax and rejuvenate. Family members or friends may be able to come in for a few hours a week, or you may want to consider hiring a care provider. Other types of assistance may include homemaker services, adult day care, Meals on Wheels, and transportation services.

You can find services in your area by going to local agencies on aging and disability, including the Eldercare Locator website maintained by the US Administration on Aging (www.eldercare.gov). The Family Caregiver Alliance (www.caregiver.org) also maintains a website where you can find information and resources for caregivers.

"Saying 'yes' to help from friends and neighbors when they offer assistance can be a blessing for everyone," Goodin says.[5] Your friends and family likely want to help, but they don't know what to do. Express what your needs are and accept help when offered.

Think about keeping a journal regarding help needed now and in the future—from grocery shopping and housework to managing finances and even providing care. Reach out to specific people suitable for these tasks.

Successfully remaining in the home environment requires substantial support from family, friends, and community. To illustrate what this success looks like, consider this scenario a recent patient encountered.

Alice was an elderly woman who was admitted to our rehabilitation unit after her second stroke. She was devastated to be in this situation again, but she had great hope for getting back home due to the hard work she and her family had done to set her up after her first stroke three years ago. In the intervening years, one of her daughters retired from working and moved into her home to provide support to her parents and help her mother with daily needs. They were able to vet and hire an excellent caregiver who came in daily from 8 a.m. to 2 p.m. to manage breakfast and lunch meals. The husband once stated that when he would look around, the caregiver was even watering the plants! They depended on her for assistance with their morning routine, including daily walks and exercises. Through occupational and physical therapy recommendations for equipment, the family was able to set up their home to accommodate Alice's needs and make caregiving easier. Access to these services makes all the difference in a patient's ability to live at home and reduce the caregiver burden so everyone in the home setting can provide loving assistance without burning out.

Have a Future Focus for Your Loved One…And for Yourself

If you are caring for a stroke survivor, you may have a lot of questions about whether your loved one will recover and what their needs will be in the months and years ahead. You may also worry about how you will manage your new role.

Caregiving is hard. At first, it will feel like a full-time job with little relief. In time, routines will settle in and life will become easier.

In the United States, more than 50 million people provide care for a loved one with a disability or illness. Up to 75 percent of caregivers are women, and most are caring for an older parent. Yet, despite the challenges of caregiving, many people report that they appreciate life more and feel positive about being able to help.

As a caregiver, it can be all too easy to make your loved one the focus of your life. Taking care of *yourself* is paramount to being able to provide care to others. You don't need to take on everything.

Here are a few items to focus on concerning your own needs.

Focus on times you can take a break. Perhaps during a home health visit, you can take a breather to walk around the block, go out for coffee with a friend, or spend some much-needed time alone. Do your best to schedule personal time. You deserve it. The more you care for yourself, the better you can care for your loved one. It's especially important not to isolate yourself, so make time to talk with and visit friends.

Focus on your physical health. Don't ignore minor health concerns, and be sure to get regularly scheduled checkups and health exams. Learn healthy ways to manage stress and relax. Eating a healthy diet, exercising regularly, and getting enough sleep will help you keep up your strength. Exhausting yourself won't allow you to provide the patient the loving help you want to give. It's not selfish to take time for your needs—it's essential, and beneficial, for both of you.

Be patient with yourself. No one is a perfect caregiver any more than they are a perfect parent. You've never done this before and will have a lot to learn.

Focus on your emotional health. Allow yourself to feel frustrated, angry, and sad, and share it with someone other than your loved one. These feeling are normal, and in order not to dwell on them, you need to express them. Here is where friends and support groups can play an important role.

Studies show that caregivers are also at risk for depression, especially if the survivor has dementia. Depression responds well to treatment, so talk with your doctor if you think you may be depressed.

Get Support. To find a support group near you, call your local hospital or do an online search for "caregiver support." You can find online support groups as well as local meetings in your area. Talking with other caregivers can help you feel less alone and provide an opportunity to share resources and caregiving tips.

Remember to laugh. Humor can be your best defense against difficult situations and feelings. You are carrying a heavy load and deserve to laugh and feel joy, so it's important to remain open to the good things life has to offer.

Summary

As you educate yourself, your ability to provide good, loving care in the home will increase. Specific knowledge about the stroke syndrome you are dealing with will empower you to have the best chance of success. Being a good caregiver is neither easy nor comfortable, yet it's critically important. Remember to take needed time for yourself. As much as possible, facilitate family and social interaction that will lead to a greater quality of life for all involved.

CHAPTER 22

WHEN END OF LIFE APPROACHES

Knowledge of our own mortality is the greatest gift God ever gave us.

— Anna Quindlen, *A Short Guide to a Happy Life*

As strong and robust as we want to believe our bodies are, the term *fragile* may be a more accurate description, especially when referring to the delicate balances in the mind. This chapter is about gaining a healthy perspective about death and the life cycle we are all in. Especially when we are young, the illusion of strength and infallibility is perhaps too enticing to resist. Even physicians struggle to reconcile this ideal of strength and fortitude with the frailty and death we so often face, both with patients and in our personal lives. However, we are all a part of the circle of life, and although a book about thriving and hope is an odd place to find a chapter about death and end of life, I would be remiss to avoid this topic. A whole book could be written on this topic, but I will just convey a few concepts.

Throughout history, the average lifespan was in the thirties or forties. Not until the last century did most people live into their older years. Especially in old age, one has to deal with dozens of "failing parts"; cartilage in the joints wears out and the joints become arthritic, proteins in the eye's lenses become yellow or cloudy, soft tissues in vessels like the aorta become calcified, and blood vessels narrow and harden, which, in turn, produces excess strain on a heart already failing to keep up with its demands that, eventually, will stop working altogether. In every man or woman, systems wear out, and in time, the person possessing these organs dies.

Medical personnel must wrestle with life and death decisions for patients, but too often, the general public doesn't think about these decisions until they are staring down the inevitable outcome of life and life's end.

The Choices Physicians Make about Their Own Deaths

It's not a frequent topic of discussion, but we doctors also eventually experience death. What is really interesting is that, by and large, we don't die like the rest of the public. What's unusual is not how much treatment we get compared to most Americans, but how *little* we choose when it's our time. For all the time we spend fending off others' deaths, we tend to be fairly serene when faced with death ourselves. We, more or less, know what is going to happen, and we know the choices because we have been to the precipice many times with many of the patients we deeply care about. When we eventually come to that point in our own lives, we generally have access to any sort of medical care we could want. But, by and large, we go gently.

A 2013 *New York Times* article brought this information to the forefront:

> When it comes to dying, doctors, of course, are ultimately no different from the rest of us. And their emotional and physical struggles are surely every bit as wrenching. But they have a clear advantage over many of us. They have seen death up close. They understand their choices, and they have access to [what] medicine has to offer.... They know enough about death to know what all people fear most: dying in pain, and dying alone.[1]

Doctors have usually talked extensively about end-of-life wishes with their families. They know, for example, that during their last moments on earth they want to avoid an unwanted CPR situation because, if done right, the CPR chest compressions will break ribs, causing them to spend their last days in an ICU, the norm for elderly patients who have had cardiac arrest.

An ongoing observational study of physicians who were medical students at the Johns Hopkins University School of Medicine between 1946 and 1964, and who have received questionnaires since then, found some interesting results. Doctors don't overtreat themselves. The questionnaire included items about whether the physicians thought their own physicians were aware of their preferences for care in the event of incapacity, and whether their spouses or family members were aware of their preferences. Most physicians reported that they would not accept CPR or other potentially life-sustaining interventions.[2] A good doctor has the responsibility to explain end-of-life options to their patients. Often this conversation involves explaining how cutting-edge technology bears on a grievously ill person near the end of life, just to keep them alive—breathing and with a pulse. The patient will be cut open, perforated with tubes, hooked up to machines, and assaulted with drugs. All of this occurs in the intensive care unit at a cost of tens of thousands of dollars a day. What it buys is misery that not many of us would choose for ourselves or our loved ones.

At the end of life, almost everyone can find a way to die in peace at home, and pain can be managed better with the right resources.

Focus on Quality of Life

Doctors who have knowledge of what may be ahead can give patients more control over their quality of life. Throughout the ages, the establishing of trust and confidence under end-of-life circumstances is a very delicate thing.

I have seen patients admitted to the hospital, having already lost consciousness, who never planned for this situation. Shocked and scared family members find themselves caught up in a maze of choices. They're overwhelmed. When doctors ask if they want "everything" done, they answer yes. Then the nightmare begins. Sometimes, a family really does mean "do everything," but often they just mean "do everything that's reasonable." For their part, doctors told to do "everything" will often do it, whether or not it is reasonable.

What the medical team and family should really be doing is focusing on what really matters—the patient's potential to recover to the point of regaining a reasonable quality of life.

Quality of life has a lot to do with our ability to maintain close relationships, and to give and receive love. Dorothy has been a patient of mine for several years, since her first stroke. She has been to my outpatient clinic numerous times, where we have chatted and talked about a whole host of things over the years, including life after stroke. (We share the experience of having a severe stroke, mine at a young age, hers in her early eighties.) At our last outpatient visit, she said, "You know, I have had close friends and peers die from stroke. I have tried to make the most of every day, because you really don't know if today will be your last." Dorothy is now eighty-five; she recently had another significant stroke and is now on my stroke rehabilitation inpatient service. The other day I had another chat with her and her family. She almost died again, yet she lives on. She maintains an optimistic attitude, despite her many impairments and challenges. My question to her was, "What makes life still worth living?" I was not surprised by her response: "I look forward to having many great experiences in the future," and those experiences centered on cherished relationships.

Dorothy's response is consistent with what I have seen as a doctor time and time again. When a reasonable potential for recovery and future relationship-building experiences exists, it's reasonable to continue aggressive care. At other times, other options should be considered.

The other day a woman came to visit me in my office. I had not seen her for a couple of years and she drove a great distance to see me. Her husband was a patient of mine who had suffered a stroke. Four years ago, he had the serious and life-threatening complication of pneumonia about three weeks after the stroke. At the time, he had to be moved from the Rehabilitation Unit to the ICU for support for his breathing. As his wife stood in my office that day, she recounted the difficult decisions she had faced several years before. She told me it was four years ago to the day that I had come to visit them in the ICU.

She came to express gratitude for giving her a fresh perspective. This good wife had faced difficult decisions at the time, including whether to choose palliative care and "letting nature take its course" or continue with aggressive medical treatments. Although palliative care is often the most compassionate course, I thought it was important to let her know about the good potential her husband had for recovery of some function and even for quality of life with her. After my visit, she decided for the course of rehabilitation that would eventually lead to recovery of function—of being able to live outside the hospital setting, walk with assistance, and take care of himself. I hoped this couple would have a few more good years together…which turned out to be the case. She told me of the many adaptations that had been necessary. He taught her that it was better to be content with your situation than to be eager and awaiting something that may never come. She had come here today to thank me for four wonderful years together, with her assuming the caregiver role, while his role in the family also shifted. She came to tell me he had recently died "a wonderful death" in her arms. This remarkable woman channeled her regrets about her husband's stroke into other fulfilling activities with her husband, while maintaining a very realistic set of expectations, including expectations about life and death. Things were not the same for either spouse after his stroke, but they chose to see the glass half full. She is a wonderful example to me, for she had the courage to choose love in spite of the worries and vulnerabilities this decision exposed.

Care Options

Research shows that most Americans do not "die well," meaning they do not die the way they say they want to—at home, surrounded by the people who love them. Only a third of patients die this way. More than 50 percent spend their final days in hospitals, often in intensive care units, tethered to machines and feeding tubes, or in nursing homes. Most people don't want to die in the ICU, as many people swallowed up by the medical establishment have spent their last days and hours.

When the time comes, palliative care and hospice care can alleviate pain and suffering, and in many cases, focus on a better quality of life near the end of life. Palliative care teams are multidisciplinary teams that work with the patient, family, and the patient's other doctors to provide medical, social, emotional, and practical support. Yet patients and families often aren't offered the hospice option, or when they are, misperceptions cause them to decide against this option.

Hospice care, which focuses on providing terminally ill patients with comfort and dignity rather than on futile cures, provides most people with much better final days. Amazingly, studies have found that people placed in hospice care often live longer than people with the same disease who are seeking active cures.

Stroke and Accepting that Life Will End

The typical recovery pattern after stroke is one of partial neurological restoration, though this comes with a lot of effort and time. However, when other circumstances are present, a more complex picture develops.

It's important to know there is a spectrum of brain dysfunction, from mild brain impairment to complete brain death. Most of the time, the cognitive deficits after stroke are subtle, but sometimes they can be severe and devastating. In cases where the stroke patient has had a form of mild or moderate dementia, when a stroke is added, the cognitive deficits are severe and permanent. In situations where the long-term outcome is less obvious, a period of waiting and monitoring for improvement is reasonable. How long to wait and monitor for improvement is a very complex and deeply personal question. Family members should consult with doctors and other healthcare providers on a frequent basis.

Years ago, when I was still early in my career, I took care of a prominent man in my hometown. With profound hemiparesis and severe swallowing problems, at eighty-six, his task of recovery and rehabilitation would not be easy. I ordered an artificial feeding tube before sending him home. The small procedure of the feeding tube placement weakened his already tenuous situation. Although I had high hopes, he went home, struggled, never recovered, and died within a few weeks. His was the first patient funeral I ever attended. Perhaps I tried to paint too rosy of a picture for the family.

With matters as delicate as life and death, it is difficult to be objective and keep emotions out of decisions, even for doctors. We do our best to keep ourselves healthy, and sometimes we recover from injuries, large and small, but eventually life must end.

Giving Yourself Permission to Let Go

At the end of life, usually well-intentioned loved ones are making decisions and calling the shots. As they, too, go through the stages of grief, like denial, anger, bargaining, etc., it is common for irrational thoughts and actions to manifest themselves. For the patient's family, the issue often becomes giving themselves permission to allow the loved one to pass. Moving on after a patient or loved one dies requires strength.

Attempting to create a higher quality of life in all of our patients often becomes an abstract goal for doctors (because doctors really cannot know what the patients' definition of quality of life is). When a patient has a severe, disabling stroke or condition, especially one with profound cognitive effects or disorders of consciousness, fostering quality of life takes on new meaning. Some of these heart-wrenchingly difficult situations can span for years. For family members affected in this way, it is often necessary to develop a new purpose with new life goals...and to find enormous strength somewhere.

As a physician, I am conscious of my obligation to not just prescribe a pill, but whenever possible, to help to heal a life. Healing comes from a sacred place within the mind. As the late neurosurgeon Dr. Paul Kalanithi, who died with his music still in him, but able to write an inspiring memoir, said, "The call to protect life—and not merely life but another's identity; it is perhaps not too much to say another's soul—[is] obvious in its sacredness.... Those burdens are what make medicine holy and wholly impossible: in taking up another's cross, one must sometimes get crushed by the weight."[3] This intersection where mortality meets immortality is a delicate thing, yet a holy thing—and death is the doorway to step through. Needless to say, it is of paramount importance to establish trust and confidence during end-of-life circumstances with all involved.

Summary

Decisions near the end of a loved one's life are difficult. When potential exists for recovery of function, the decision to take aggressive steps is reasonable. Potential for recovering quality of life may be best defined as a hope for great experiences in the future and a focus on relationships with others. If that potential for recovery ceases, it becomes important, though usually difficult, to give yourself permission to be at peace with letting go.

A FINAL NOTE:

THE ADAPTIVE SPIRAL REVISITED

*We shall not cease from exploration
And the end of all our exploring
Will be to arrive where we started
And know the place for the first time.*

— T. S. Eliot, "Little Gidding"

A few years ago, I did a long radio interview. Some people have joked, "You have a face for the radio." I thought, since speaking is not my strong suit, maybe I have a voice for books. Although public speaking is an important part of my responsibilities, I may not have written two books if I were a strong speaker. Stroke has made me adapt—possibly in ways that push me to do things I wouldn't do otherwise—and forced my life to blossom into something sweet.

This book is about the struggles I and multitudes of others have had with stroke, but the challenges and efforts to overcome stroke can be superimposed on any number of less severe and commonplace problems we all encounter. Although it's not possible nor appropriate to superimpose my experience with stroke on all stroke patients, I hope you take pertinent elements from my story. In his book *Crow and Weasel*, Barry Lopez says that "stories people tell have a way of taking care of them. If stories come to you, care for them. And learn to give them away when they are needed. Sometimes a person needs a story more than food to stay alive. This is why we put these stories in each other's memories. This is how people care for themselves."[1] Sometimes, that story is merely in reminding an individual of past successes, while at other times it comes in the form of another person's experience. Both can be powerful; both are important.

My purpose has been to outline guidelines for you to use in various situations since each stroke is unique and different. An overarching theme, which I deeply believe in, has been the concept of the adaptive spiral. If there is a purpose to life (and I think there is), it is that through our struggles, painful though they may be, we can grow and develop as human beings. If you believe in a Higher Power, perhaps this belief strengthens you, including when in the midst of struggles. I know struggles are universal to the human experience. Mine is a story of a journey through devastation, a journey to find understanding, hope, and purpose. My experience is not at all unique, but speaks to broad and basic truths that apply to each of us, even through hardship and strife.

Perhaps, even though we struggle, we carry boundless potential, made possible *because* we struggle—which is the real work of our lives. We can find the meaning in struggles or even in pain and suffering, if we have the strength to choose it. Our struggles take on new meaning when they meet purpose. For, despite whatever has happened, you still have a choice.

The human body and spirit are incredibly resilient. We can all overcome hard things. When we focus our energy and attention on things that will truly bring greater function for the purpose of greater quality of life, we can obtain or regain a greater sense of happiness. Universal factors are related to quality of life and happiness, but those factors are not what most people automatically think of. Happiness comes down, in a very real sense, to the ability to give and receive love. For people who have had stroke, or any number of other challenges, the struggle is to regain health and then live to obtain a high quality of life. In most cases, this process is very action-oriented and does not happen without very intentional effort.

You and your family are on a journey. I hope this book helps navigate and guide you through the process.

Since the firestorm of my stroke—and because of it—my life has been full of opportunities for growth, joy, and love. And I am thankful. Life can become so much more than a fight to regain function and independence or a struggle to reclaim quality of life. Life's struggles become part of our life stories, but those life stories have less to do with the struggles, and more to do with connecting with others.

Our human minds and bodies are limited and imperfect, yet one characteristic of them is that we can improve and change through purposeful effort. It's as if we are built of clay, having the ability to be molded, which offers every human the opportunity to be shaped by experience, by choice, and by the only brain we have. The human mind and body do not have a flawed design; rather, they should be celebrated as the means for growth to reach our potential.

My hope is that you can focus on quality of life, despite life's hardships—that you can confidently act and face whatever comes your way. Nothing can be accomplished without action and power, but first one has to choose to believe they can succeed. Hard questions remain, including those at the end of life. Human suffering, from stroke, depression, cancer, heart disease, or any number of things our human bodies are susceptible to, invariably cause suffering, struggles, and sometimes death…. We are all products of our biology, physiology, and psychology—our human bodies.

However, cultivating true happiness—happiness that touches us so we can achieve a higher quality of life—is a goal many people seek. Our ability to gain true and lasting happiness stems from our ability to build loving relationships. Happiness is also heavily influenced by our expectations: what we think about what the world gives us and how life should behave. Happiness is about channeling our response through believing in ourselves, choosing to transform our regrets, and finding fulfillment in other activities.

As I said before, if you are on the right track, it is going to be uphill. It may not be an unbearably steep climb, but pushing ourselves to improve, adapt, and grow, even in the face of severe challenges, is one of the critical components to attaining happiness and a high quality of life.

C. S. Lewis insightfully wrote:

> That is what mortals misunderstand. They say of some temporal suffering, 'No future bliss can make up for it,' not knowing that Heaven, once attained, will work backwards and turn even that agony into a glory.... And that is why, at the end of all things, when the sun rises here...the blessed will say, 'We have never lived anywhere except in Heaven.'[2]

I wish nothing but the best for you along life's journey; I hope it is filled with joy and happiness, even though you may also experience pain and hardship. May your bitter struggles turn into your noblest victories.

BIBLIOGRAPHY

Baldwin, C. et al. "The effect of vocational rehabilitation on return to work rates post-stroke: a systematic review." *Top Stroke Rehabil.* 18(5), (2011): 562-572.

Bauby, J. D. *The Diving Bell and the Butterfly.* Paris, France: Editions Rorbert Laffont, 1997.

Bono, E. D. *Six Thinking Hats.* New York: Little Brown and Company, 1985.

Broderick, C. *The Uses of Adversity.* Salt Lake City: Deseret Book Company, 2008.

Brown, Brené. *Daring Greatly: How the Courage to Be Vulnerable Transforms the Way We Live and Lead.* New York: Penguin Random House, 2012.

Brown, Brené. "The power of vulernerability." www.ted.com. (June 2010). Retrieved from https://www.ted.com/talks/brene_brown_on_vulnerability.

Bush, George W. "A Day of Terror: Bush's Remarks to the Nation on the Terrorist Attacks." *New York Times.* September 12, 2001. Retrieved from: https://www.nytimes.com/2001/09/12/us/a-day-of-terror-bush-s-remarks-to-the-nation-on-the-terrorist-attacks.html.

Camping Magazine. "The Restorative Powers of Nature: An Interview with Florence Williams." January 22, 2019. Retrieved from www.acacamps.org: https://www.acacamps.org/resource-library/camping-magazine/restorative-powers-nature.

Covey, Stephen R. *The Seven Habits of Highly Effective People.* New York: Simon & Schuster, 1989.

Davidson, R. *The Emotional Life of Your Brain.* New York: Plume, 2012.

Davidson, R. "The Science of a Happy Mind, Part 1." *National Geographic.* (February 2018). Retrieved from https://video.national geographic.com/video/ng live/160321-davidson-healthy-mind-part1-lecture-nglive.

Donald, M. *Origins of the Modern Mind.* Boston: Harvard UP, 1991.

Edgley, Steven R. "Stroke and neurodegenerative disorders: community integration." *PM&R* (March 2009): 527-34.

Erikson, Erik. *The Life Cycle Completed: Extended Version.* New York: W.W. Norton, 1998.

Frankl, Victor. *Man's Search for Meaning.* New York: Beacon Press, 2006.

Frost, Robert. *The Poetry of Robert Frost: Stopping by Wood on a Snowy Evening.* New York: Holt, Rinehart, and Winston, 1969.

Gallo, Joseph J. "Life-Sustaining Treatments: What Do Physicians Want and Do They Express Their Wishes to Others?" *Journal of the American Geriatrics Society.* 51(2003): 961–69.

Gilbert, Daniel. *Stumbling on Happiness.* New York: Vintage Books, 2007.

Goldstein, LB, et al. "Primary prevention of ischemic stroke." *Circulation.* (2006)

Gombrich, E. *A Little History of the World.* New Haven: Yale UP, 1985.

Gordon NF, et al. Physical activity and exercise recommendations for stroke survivors. *Stroke* 109(16), (2004): 2031-2041.

Gorenstein, D. "How Doctors Die: Showing Others the Way." *The New York Times.* November 19, 2013.

Greitens, E. *Resilience.* New York: Mariner Books, 2015.

Hemingway, Ernest. *A Farewell to Arms.* New York: Scribner, 1929.

Joseph, S. *What Doesn't Kill Us: The New Psychology of Posttraumatic Growth.* New York: Basic Books, 2011.

Kalanithi, P. *When Breath Becomes Air.* New York: Random House, 2016.

Kaufman, B. *The Post-Presidency from Washington to Clinton.* Lawrence, KS: UP of Kansas, 2012.

Kennedy, J. F. Retrieved July 31, 2018 from Quotable Quotes: https://www.goodreads.com/quotes/493205-we-choose-to-go-to-the-moon-in-this-decade.

Kübler-Ross, Elisabeth. *On Grief and Grieving.* New York: Scribner, 2005.

Kushner, Harold. *When Bad Things Happen to Good People.* New York: Schocken Books, 1981.

Lewis, C. S. *The Great Divorce, a Dream.* San Francisco: Harper, 1946.

Lewis, C. S. *Mere Christianity.* New York: MacMillan, 1952.

Licht, S. *Stroke and Its Rehabilitation.* Baltimore: Waverly Press, 1975.

Lynberg, M. *Make Each Day Your Masterpiece.* Kansas City: Andrews McMeel, 2001.

Marshall, S. C. "Predictors of driving ability following stroke: a systematic review." *Top Stroke Rehabil.* 14(1), (Jan-Feb 2007): 98-114.

McGrath, C., et al. "Post-traumatic growth in acquired brain injury: A preliminary small scale study." *Brain Injury.* 20(7), (2006): 767-73.

O'Leary, V. & Ickovics, J. "Resilience and thriving in response to challenge: an opportunity for a paradigm shift in women's health." *Women's Health.* (1995): 121-42.

Oliver, M. *Winter Hours: Prose, Prose Poems, and Poems.* Boston: Houghon Mifflin Company, 1999.

Quindlen, Anna. *A Short Guide to a Happy Life.* New York: Random House, 2000.

Ruttens-Jacobs, C., et al. "Long-Term Mortality After Stroke Among Adults Aged 18 to 50 Years." *JAMA.* 308(11), (2013): 1136-44.

Salter, K. *Community Reintegration.* Retrieved September 10, 2008 from The Evidence-Based Review of Stroke Rehabilitation: www.ebrsr.com.

Fisher, M., et al. "Nutrition and stroke prevention." *Stroke.* 37(9), (2006): 2430-35.

Teasell, R. *Clinical Consequences of Stroke.* Retrieved March 2018 from Evidence-Based Review of Stroke Rehabilitation: http://www.ebrsr.com/sites/default/files/v18-SREBR-CH2-NET.pdf.

Tedeschi, L. C. *The Handbook of Posttraumatic Growth: Research and Practice.* New York: Psychology Press, 2014.

Tedeshi, R. *Posttraumatic Growth: Conceptual Foundation and Empirical Evidence.* Philadelphia: Lawrence Erlbaum Associates, 2004.

Thoreau, Henry David. *Walden, or, Life in the Woods.* 1854. New York: E.P. Dutton, 1908.

Tyson, J., et al. "Turning a tragedy into a tribute: A literature review of creating meaning after loss of a loved one." *Illness, Crisis, & Loss.* 21(4), (2013): 325-340.

Waldinder, R. "Becoming Wise." *TED Radio Hour.* National Public Radio. Retrieved June 10, 2016 from www.npr.org/programs/ted-radio-hour/481290551/becoming-wise.

Watkins CL, et al. "Prevalence of spasticity post stroke." *Clin Rehabil.* 16(5) (2002): 515-522.

Weng, H., et al. "Compassion Training Alters Altruism and Neural Responses to Suffering." *Psychological Science.* 24(7), (2013): 1171-80.

Whitman, Walt. "Manly Health and Training, with Off-Hand Hints Toward Their Conditions." *Walt Whitman Quarterly Review.* 33 (2016): 212.

Williams, Florence. *The Nature Fix.* New York: W.W. Norton, 2017.

END NOTES

Chapter 2: Silence

1. Gombrich, E. *A Little History of the World*. New Haven: Yale UP, 1985. p. 187.
2. Bono, E. D. *Six Thinking Hats*. New York: Little Brown and Company, 1985. p. 34.
3. Kushner, Harold. *When Bad Things Happen to Good People*. New York: Schocken Books, 1981. p. 60-61.
4. Lynberg, M. *Make Each Day Your Masterpiece*. Kansas City: Andrews McMeel, 2001. p. 7.
5. Frost, Robert. *The Poetry of Robert Frost: Stopping by Wood on a Snowy Evening*. New York: Holt, Rinehart, and Winston, 1969.

Chapter 3: Doing the Hard Things and Rising

1. Kennedy, J. F. Retrieved July 31, 2018 from Quotable Quotes: https://www.goodreads.com/quotes/493205-we-choose-to-go-to-the-moon-in-this-decade.
2. Bush, George W. "A Day of Terror: Bush's Remarks to the Nation on the Terrorist Attacks." *New York Times*. September 12, 2001. Retrieved from: https://www.nytimes.com/2001/09/12/us/a-day-of-terror-bush-s-remarks-to-the-nation-on-the-terrorist-attacks.html.

Chapter 4: Conquering the Mind

1. Covey, Stephen R. *The Seven Habits of Highly Effective People*. New York: Simon & Schuster, 1989. p. 23.
2. Lynberg, M. *Make Each Day Your Masterpiece*. Kansas City: Andrews McMeel, 2001. p. 28.

Chapter 5: When a Door Closes, Build a New One

1. Lewis, C. S. *Mere Christianity*. New York: MacMillan, 1952. p. 176.
2. Tedeshi, R. *Posttraumatic Growth: Conceptual Foundation and Empirical Evidence*. Philadelphia: Lawrence Erlbaum Associates, 2004.
3. McGrath, C., et al. "Post-traumatic growth in acquired brain injury: A preliminary small scale study." *Brain Injury*. (2006): p. 767-73.
4. Ibid.
5. Salter, K. *Community Reintegration*. Retrieved September 10, 2008 from *The Evidence-Based Review of Stroke Rehabilitation*: www.ebrsr.com.
6. Tedeschi, L. C. *The Handbook of Posttraumatic Growth: Research and Practice*. New York: Psychology Press, 2014.

Chapter 6: Hunter and Prey

1. Frankl, Victor. *Man's Search for Meaning*. New York: Beacon Press, 2006. p. 88.
2. Ibid.
3. O'Leary, V. & Ickovics, J. "Resilience and thriving in response to challenge: an opportunity for a paradigm shift in women's health." *Women's Health*. (1995): 121-42.
4. McGrath, C., et al. "Post-traumatic growth in acquired brain injury: A preliminary small scale study." *Brain Injury*. (2006): 767-73.

Chapter 7: What Is "Stroke"? Demystifying the Myths

1. Licht, S. *Stroke and Its Rehabilitation*. Baltimore: Waverly Press, 1975. p. 12.
2. Ibid.
3. Jennifer Majersik. Personal Interview. June 3, 2019.
4. Broderick, C. *The Uses of Adversity*. Salt Lake City: Deseret Book Company, 2008. p. 7.

Chapter 8: Prevention and New Frontiers

1. Goldstein, L.B. et al. "Primary prevention of ischemic stroke." *Circulation*. (2006)
2. Fisher, M., et al. "Nutrition and stroke prevention." *Stroke*. 37(9), (2006): 2430-35.
3. Gordon, N. F. et al. Physical activity and exercise recommendations for stroke survivors. *Stroke*. 109(16), (2004): 2031-2041.
4. Covey, Stephen R. *The Seven Habits of Highly Effective People*. New York: Simon & Schuster, 1989. p. 288.

Chapter 9: Language Center: The Rocket Scientist and the Eloquent Tissue of the Brain

1. Donald, M. *Origins of the Modern Mind*. Boston: Harvard UP, 1991.

Chapter 11: Cognitive Syndromes After Stroke: Right Brain Syndromes

1. Teasell, R. *Clinical Consequences of Stroke*. Retrieved March 2018 from Evidence-Based Review of Stroke Rehabilitation: http://www.ebrsr.com/sites/default/files/v18-SREBR-CH2-NET.pdf.
2. Kaufman, B. *The Post-Presidency from Washington to Clinton*. Lawrence, Kansas: UP of Kansas, 2012. p. 264.

Chapter 12: Despite Chance Events, You Can Make Your Mark

1. Bauby, J. D. *The Driving Bell and the Butterfly*. Paris, France: Editions Rorbert Laffont, 1997. p. 131.

Chapter 13: Surrounding Yourself With Great Resources: Critical Collaborations

1. Covey, Stephen R. *The Seven Habits of Highly Effective People*. New York: Simon & Schuster, 1989. p. 216.

2. Gallo, Joseph J. "Life-Sustaining Treatments: What Do Physicians Want and Do They Express Their Wishes to Others?" *Journal of the American Geriatrics Society*. 51(2003): p. 175-76.

Chapter 15: Adaptive Spiral and the Plastic Brain

1. Harvey, Richard L. Personal Interview. April 14, 2011.
2. Brown, Brené. *Daring Greatly: How the Courage to Be Vulnerable Transforms the Way We Live and Lead*. New York: Penguin Random House, 2012: p.69, 73.

Chapter 16: Spasticity and the Freedom to Move

1. Watkins, C. L. et al. "Prevalence of spasticity post stroke." *Clin Rehabil.* (2002) 16(5): 515-522.

Chapter 17: Stroke in the Young: Unique Issues of Driving, Working, and Other Aspects

1. Ruttens-Jacobs, C. et al. "Long-Term Mortality After Stroke Among Adults Aged 18 to 50 Years." *JAMA*. 308(11), (2013): 1136-44.
2. Marshall, S. C. et al. "Predictors of driving ability following stroke: a systematic review." *Top Stroke Rehabil*. 14(1), (Jan-Feb 2007): 98-114.
3. Baldwin, C. et al. "The effect of vocational rehabilitation on return to work rates post-stroke: a systematic review." *Top Stroke Rehabil*. 18(5), (2011): 562-572.
4. Edgley, S. R., et al. "Stroke and neurodegenerative disorders: community integration." *PM&R* (March 2009): 527-34.

Chapter 18: Stages of Life and Loss, and the Potential to Repurpose Loss for Good

1. Erikson, Erik. *The Life Cycle Completed: Extended Version*. New York: W.W. Norton, 1998. p. 110-11.

2. Ibid.
3. Ibid.
4. Kübler-Ross, Elisabeth. *On Grief and Grieving*. New York: Scribner, 2005. p. 7-24.
5. Ibid.
6. Brown, Brené. "The power of vulernerability." www.ted.com. (June 2010). Retrieved from https://www.ted.com/talks/brene_brown_on_vulnerability.
7. Davidson, R. *The Emotional Life of Your Brain*. New York: Plume, 2012. p. 104.
8. Gilbert, Daniel. *Stumbling on Happiness*. New York: Vintage Books, 2007.
9. Lynberg, M. *Make Each Day Your Masterpiece*. Kansas City: Andrews McMeel, 2001. p. 96.
10. Davidson, R. "The Science of a Happy Mind, Part 1." *National Geographic*. (February 2018). Retrieved from https://video.nationalgeographic.com/video/ng live/160321-davidson-healthy-mind-part1-lecture-nglive.
11. Ibid.
12. Weng, H., et al. "Compassion Training Alters Altruism and Neural Responses to Suffering." *Psychological Science*. 24(7), (2013): 1171-80.

Chapter 19: Resilience

1. Greitens, E. *Resilience*. New York: Mariner Books, 2015. p. 3.
2. Ibid.
3. McGrath, C., et al. "Post-traumatic growth in acquired brain injury: A preliminary small scale study." *Brain Injury*. 20(7), (2006): 767-73.
4. Tyson, J. "Turning a tragedy into a tribute: A literature review of creating meaning after loss of a loved one." *Illness, Crisis, & Loss*. 21(4), (2013): 325-340.
5. Tedeshi, R. *Posttraumatic Growth: Conceptual Foundation and Em-

pirical Evidence. Philadelphia: Lawrence Erlbaum Associates, 2004.
6. Waldinder, R. "Becoming Wise." TED Radio Hour. National Public Radio. Retrieved June 10, 2016 from www.npr.org/programs/ted-radio-hour/481290551/becoming-wise.
7. Salter, K. *Community Reintegration*. Retrieved September 10, 2008 from The Evidence-Based Review of Stroke Rehabilitation: www.ebrsr.com.
8. Hemingway, Ernest. *A Farewell to Arms*. New York: Scribner, 1929.

Chapter 20: Nature's Restorative Power
1. Williams, Florence. *The Nature Fix*. New York: W.W. Norton, 2017.
2. "The Restorative Powers of Nature: An Interview with Florence Williams." *Camping Magazine*. January 22, 2019. Retrieved from www.acacamps.org: https://www.acacamps.org/resource-library/camping-magazine/restorative-powers-nature.
3. Williams, Florence. *The Nature Fix*. New York: W.W. Norton, 2017. p. 190.
4. Ibid.
5. Thoreau, Henry David. *Walden, or, Life in the Woods*. 1854. New York: E.P. Dutton, 1908.
6. Williams, Florence. *The Nature Fix*. New York: W.W. Norton, 2017. p. 194.
7. Jeffrey Rosenbluth and Tanja Kari. Personal Interview. March 21, 2019.
8. Anonymous Patient. Personal Interview. April 5, 2019.

Chapter 21: Caregivers of Stroke Patients: Unsung Heroes
1. Pat Goodin. Personal Interview. February 20, 2019.
2. Ibid.
3. Ibid.
4. Ibid.
5. Ibid.

Chapter 22: When End of Life Approaches

1. Gorenstein, D. "How Doctors Die: Showing Others the Way." *The New York Times*. November 19, 2013.
2. Gallo, Joseph J. "Life-Sustaining Treatments: What Do Physicians Want and Do They Express Their Wishes to Others?" *Journal of the American Geriatrics Society*. 51(2003): 175-76.
3. Kalanithi, P. *When Breath Becomes Air*. New York: Random House, 2016. p. 98.

A Final Note: The Adaptive Spiral Revisited

1. Lopez, Barry. *Crow and Weasel*. New York: Square Fish, 1998. p. 62.
2. Lewis, C. S. *The Great Divorce, a Dream*. San Francisco: Harper, 1946.

INDEX

A

Abdominal obesity, 85

Abulia, 132

Acceptance, 34, 180, 182, 244

Achievement, 65, 70, 134, 159

Active struggle and slow rising, 145

Adaptive recreation, 89, 179, 192, 198, 200

Adaptive spiral, 20, 65, 69, 127, 133, 145, 149, 190, 201, 205, 221

Aerobic exercise, 61, 193

Alcohol, 85, 166

Americans with Disabilities Act, 175

Amphetamines, 85

Aneurysm, 166

Anger, 34, 36, 181, 184, 219

Anterior cerebral artery, 177

Anxiety, 103, 131, 167, 174, 178, 195, 199

Apoplexy, 74, 75

Arterial dissection, 192

Arteriovenous malformation (avm) rupture, 166

Artery of Percheron, 118

Aspiration, 139

Ataxia, 119, 120, 122

Atrial fibrillation, 84, 177

Attention Restoration Theory, 195

B

Baclofen, 160, 161, 163

Bargaining, 34, 182, 219

Basilar artery, 120

Bauby, Jean-Dominique, 120, 121

Beecher, Henry Ward, 23

Body mass index, 85

Bolte, Jill, 95

Botulinum toxin injections, 142, 160

Brainstem, 108, 120, 193

Broca, Paul, 93, 94, 95, 97

Broca's aphasia, 93, 94, 95, 97

Broderick, Carlfred, 79

Brown, Brené, 149, 183

Bush, George W., 39

C

Caregivers, 101, 105, 112, 203

Carotid artery, 192

Central neuropathic pain, 140

Cerebellum, 119, 120

Cerebral cortex, 107, 108

Chicago Marathon, 54

Cholesterol, 85, 86, 89, 117, 166

Circle of Willis, 75

Clinical assessment, 133, 159

Cocaine, 85

Cognitive deficits, 140, 171, 219

Coming home, 207

Competency, 65, 69

Complications of stroke, 137, 155

Confucius, 107

Constraint-induced movement therapy (cimt), 151

Couch factor, 88

Covey, Stephen R., 1, 47, 88, 126, 165

Cowboy poet, 99, 102

Craig H. Neilsen Rehabilitation Hospital, 199

Cretan Mediterranean diet, 86

Crow and Weasel, 221

D

Dantrolene sodium, 160

Davidson, Richard, 184, 185

de Bono, Edward, 34

Deep venous thrombosis, 139

Dehydration and fluid management, 142

Denial, 34, 181, 219,

Depression, 143, 174, 182, 207, 210

Diabetes mellitus, 85, 168

Diaschisis, 146

Diazepam, 160

Dickens, Charles, 203

Donald, Merlin, 92

Dorian, Emil, 187

Dreher, Henry, 184

Driving, 112, 165, 167

E

Edgley, Marcia, 67

Einstein, Albert, 37,

Eliot, T. S., 221

Eloquent tissue, 52, 91

Emboli/embolus, 75, 139

Emerson, Ralph Waldo, 47

Employment, 166, 170, 174
End of life, 213
Erikson, Erik, 178, 180
Exercise, 61, 68, 85, 143, 156, 167, 193, 195, 201
Exploration, 65, 68
Expressive aphasia, 94, 170

F
Falls, 109, 119, 140, 207
Fluent aphasia, 103
Four horsemen, 130
Frankl, Victor, 64
Frog 137, 140
Frost, Robert, 37
Functional progress, 134, 159

G
Glass half-full, 189
Goal setting, 48, 133, 159
Goodin, Pat, 205,
Gorilla, 137, 138
Governing center, 107, 109
Greitens, Eric, 187

H
Halevi, Yehuda, 183
Harvesting hope, 126
Hebb, Donald, 147
Hemingway, Ernest, 194
Hemiplegic shoulder pain, 132, 141
Hemorrhagic stroke, 76, 94, 166
Hemorrhagic transformation, 139
Heroin, 85
Herschel, Abraham Joshua, 91
Hospice care, 218
Human spirituality
Hypercoagulable state, 35
Hypertension, 75, 83, 85, 166

I
Identifying change, 127
Intrathecal baclofen pump, 161
Ischemic stroke, 75, 85

J
James, William, 145
Jesuit, 31, 32, 34
Joseph, Stephen, 126

K

Kari, Tanja, 199
Keller, Helen, 48, 186,
Kennedy, John F., 39
King, Martin Luther, Jr., 71
Kipling, Rudyard, 31
Kübler-Ross model 33, 81, 181
Kushner, Harold, 36

L

Language as art, 99
Learned non-use, 151
Left middle cerebral artery, 97, 101
Lewis, C. S., 57, 224
Lieberman, Phillip, 93
Limbic system, 97, 108
Locked-in syndrome, 120
Lopez, Barry, 221
Loyola Medical School, 31

M

Majersik, Jennifer, 77
Maladaptive spiral, 65, 87, 123, 138, 141
Marriage, 179, 203,
Meditation, 61
Migraines, 166
Mindfulness, 61
Motivation, 65, 66, 131
Murakami, Haruki, 155
Mustard seed, 66, 68

N

Nature 194, 195
Neurologic restoration, 43, 129
Neurological neglect, 111, 113
Neurological reorganization, 147
Neuropathic pain, 132, 140
Non-fluent aphasia, 94,

O

Obesity, 85, 88
Oliver, Mary, 39
Oral contraceptives, 84
Origins of the modern mind, 92

P

Paradigm, 47, 57, 73, 88
Paralympic games, 199
Patent foramen ovale, 118
Phenol (alcohol) injections, 160,

161

Physical medicine and rehabilitation, 79

Plasticity, 52, 145,

Polio, 67

Poor arousal, 131

Poor mood, 88, 131, 156

Poor motivation and despondency, 132

Post-traumatic growth, 191

Prayer, 61

Prepare yourself financially, 205

Pulmonary embolism, 139

R

Range of caregiving needs, 206

Re-authoring, 127

Receptive aphasia, 100, 101

Recurrent stroke, 87, 139

Rehabilitation triage, 128

Resilience, 120, 126, 187

Resilient, 184, 187, 191, 194

Resurrection Hospital, 42, 59

Return to work, 53, 70, 120, 167, 170, 174

Right middle cerebral artery, 112, 172

Risk factors, 82, 83, 84, 87, 166, 208,

Rosenbluth, Jeffrey, 199

S

Safety, 39, 104, 167

Sapling, 153

Schweitzer, Albert, 57, 125

Scott, Victoria, 63

Secondary prevention, 83, 86

Seizures, 139

Setterfield, Diane, 99

Shakespeare, William, 47

Shame, 78, 79, 87, 143, 149, 156, 171, 198

Shoulder subluxation, 141

Smoking, 84, 88, 102, 166

Spastic bladder, 143

Spasticity, 133, 142, 144, 155-164

Spasticity and hypertonia, 133, 142, 144, 155-164

Spontaneous recovery, 146

Stages of life, 177

Static or dynamic splints, 160

Strauss, Robert, 137

Strayer, David, 197

Stress-Reduction Theory, 195

Stroke in the young, 165

Stroke of Insight, 95

Sub-cortical brain structures, 107

Succumbing, 64

Superstitious, 74

Support groups, 143, 171, 179, 192, 205, 210

Surviving, 64

Swallowing problems, 122, 138

T

Task-specific, repetitive, goal-oriented practice, 149

Telestroke, 77

The Nature Fix, 195

The Six Thinking Hats, 34

Thoreau, Henry David, 53, 62, 196, 198

Thrombectomy, 76

Thrombus, 75

Tissue plasminogen activator, 76

Tizanidine, 160

TRAILS (Technology Recreation Access Independence Lifestyle Sports), 198, 199

Treatment for spasticity, 159

Turkle, Sherry, 197

U

University of Utah Medical Center, 188

Urinary tract infection, 140

V

Valuing change, 127

Vertebral artery, 119

Vertigo, 119, 120, 122

Vocational rehabilitation program, 175, 180

Vulnerability, 185, 186

W

Waldinder, Robert, 192

Walking ability and walking speed, 144

Wallenberg's syndrome, 121, 122, 123

Wepfer, Johann Jakob, 74

Wernicke, Carl, 100

Wernicke's aphasia, 99, 100, 101, 103, 104

ABOUT THE AUTHOR

Steven Edgley is an Associate Professor in the Division of Physical Medicine and Rehabilitation and the Director of Stroke Rehabilitation at the University of Utah. At age twenty-eight, he survived a massive stroke. Today, he is involved with both the clinical aspects of stroke rehabilitation and with research on new techniques and methods to promote, facilitate, and improve life after stroke. His aim is to help patients through clinical care and practical applications to achieve greater independence and quality of life after stroke.

Dr. Edgley graduated from Brigham Young University in 1997, with medical school completion at Loyola University in Chicago in 2001. He completed his residency in Physical Medicine and Rehabilitation in 2006 at the University of Utah in Salt Lake City, and received his board certification with the American Board of Physical Medicine and Rehabilitation in 2007. In 2013, Dr. Edgley was given the Healthcare Hero Award by *Utah Business Magazine* for his advocacy of stroke patients, which is inspired by his personal experience. He and his wife Emi live in Salt Lake City and are the parents of two daughters, Ella and Louisa. In his free time, he enjoys hiking, skiing, waterskiing, and cycling.

IF YOU BENEFITED FROM *THRIVING AFTER YOUR STROKE,* DON'T MISS READING *LIFE BETWEEN TWO GARDENS*

Experiencing challenges, being broken, and having to pick up the pieces of our lives is part of the human condition. Eventually, we learn how to fit those pieces back together so they make sense, we are stronger, and our faith becomes greater.

Steven Edgley knows about putting the pieces back together after experiencing a devastating life event. As a stroke survivor, he has written *Life Between Two Gardens* to record his amazing journey of survival, recovery, and faith in the Lord. His story of overcoming a stroke serves as a metaphor for overcoming whatever challenges we all face in life.

In these pages, you will find words of comfort and reassurance that a loving God is intimately aware of our individual circumstances and will provide tender support for our needs. Even though there may be hardship, strife, and even evil cast around us, and times of darkness when we cry out for a lantern to guide the way, we will eventually see that it is the Father's love that built this stage called earth. We are actors on this stage, living life in the frame between two important gardens—

the Garden of Eden, which set the stage for our subsequent evolving purpose, hope, and joy in our Redeemer, and which culminated in the Garden of Gethsemane.

On this stage we learn the lessons we most need to prepare us for the next aspect of our eternal lives. Steven Edgley invites you to share some of your stage time with him. You will come to marvel with him over how the Lord allows us to be strengthened in surprising ways, and you will ultimately be empowered to act and achieve in ways only you and the Lord can envision for your life.

Get your copy of *Life Between Two Gardens* today at www.LifeBetweenTwoGardens.com.

BOOK STEVEN EDGLEY
TO SPEAK AT YOUR NEXT EVENT

Dr. Steven Edgley has extensive speaking experience at local, national, and international venues. He is available to speak at conventions, conferences, and meetings. Steven can connect with an audience through personal, inspirational stories, backed by cutting-edge scientific and medical information.

If you want to book Steven Edgley to speak, contact him directly with the contact information below:

801.833.7457

Steve.Edgley@gmail.com

www.ThrivingAfterYourStroke.com